WHY, YOU CHEEKY YOUNG SCOUNDRELS! I'LL SHOW Y
WHO'S BOSS HERE! JUST FOR THAT I'LL DRAW THE
GASWORKS GANG INSTEAD OF YOU FOR THE 'BEAN
HO!! STOP SHOVING!
COME THROUGH TO THE LOUNGE FOR A CUP OF TEA, BOYS. I'LL FINISH THE CARTOON AFTERWARDS!
GEE, THANKS!
NOW'S MY CHANCE TO TAKE WATTY'S CARTOON AWAY AND LEAVE MINE INSTEAD!
BACK IN TH
DO YOU MIND IF WE HAVE A LOO AT THE CARTOO MR WATKIN
AW A ON TOO— IT WON'T THE KIND OSE TOUGHS ILL LIKE!
AF477065

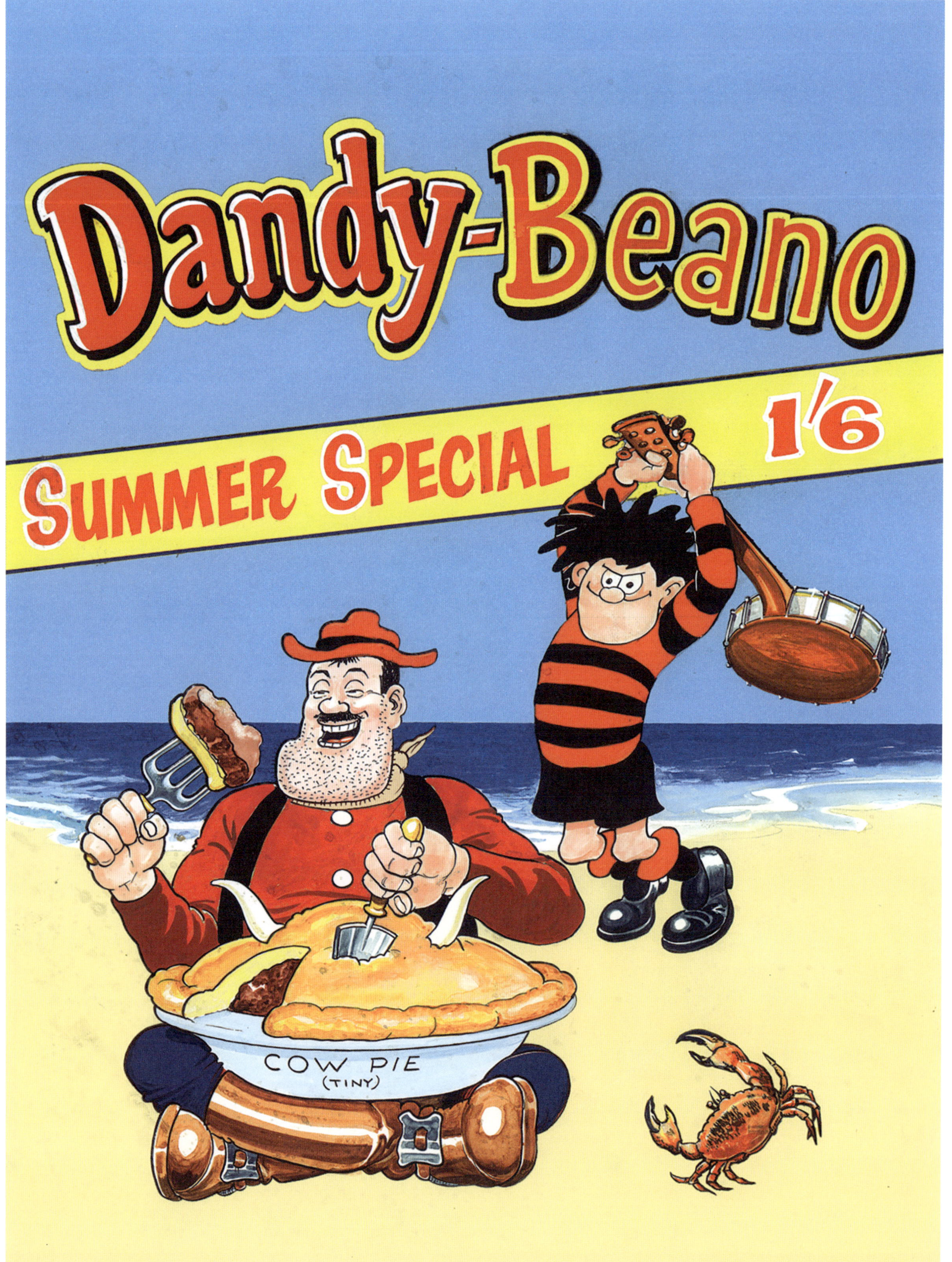
Dandy-Beano
SUMMER SPECIAL
1'6
COW PIE
(TINY)

Celebrating one of DC Thomson's most beloved and best known artists, Dudley D Watkins is renowned for his work on some of their most prestigious titles. With a talent for visual humour in comic strips and an uncanny eye for detail, here we've collected some of his greatest works.

Watkins' long career saw him work not only on Oor Wullie and The Broons, but many other classics such as Lord Snooty, Desperate Dan and Jimmy and his Magic Patch — to name but a few! With such an array of material from such a prolific artist, there's certain to be plenty of laughs from this comic strip legend.

DCT Consumer Products (UK) Ltd. 2020
D.C. Thomson and Co. Ltd.,
185 Fleet Street,
London EC4A 2HS.

Printed in the EU.

1930s

Although Dudley D Watkins' career began at DC Thomson in 1925, he didn't truly find himself embroiled in comic capers until 1933 when he began work on The Rover Midget Comic and The Skipper Midget Comic in 1934. From there, Watkins snowballed into regular cartoon work, landing himself his first regular strip a year later in the form of the puntastic Percy Vere and His Trying Tricks — a young magician whose tricks often went hilariously awry.

With his new-found experience regularly drawing wee scamps and naughty children, it's no surprise that in 1936, Watkins was approached to co-create and illustrate his most enduring characters; the highly rambunctious Scottish institutions, Oor Wullie and The Broons.

Following on from this, The Dandy was launched in 1937 and Watkins was asked to draw the roughest, toughest, cow pie loving cowboy in the West, Desperate Dan, along with the cantankerous old coot, Smarty Grandpa. The Dandy was followed shortly the next year by Beano, which Watkins was also asked to contribute to, this time picking up the upper-class rascal, Lord Snooty.

And this was just the beginning of what would become a comics career spanning forty years...

THE BROONS &
OOR WULLIE

Dudley D Watkins' most famous characters, The Broons and Oor Wullie, have been a staple of The Sunday Post since 1936.

Watkins drew editor RD Low's laconically Scots creations for the Fun Section of the institutional Dundee paper until the late 1960s. During his three decade run, Watkins' style settled in the first couple of years and the characters have barely changed since, cementing the look of the dungaree-clad scamp and loving yet dysfunctional family.

To this day, the yearly Broons and Oor Wullie giftbook and annual are a welcome sight in many a home.

THE SUNDAY POST
FUN SECTION
'OOR WULLIE'
AH'M FED UP! I NEVER GET ONY FUN HERE.
WHISTLE ??
FIRE BRIGADE
FIRE ALARM PRESS
FIRE ALARM PRESS
RING ?? DING
BANK
FINE DAY
AH'M FED UP! I NEVER GET ONY FUN HERE.

When Wullie Visited Aunt Mabel
He Was Just As Good As He Was Able.

Though Wullie's Ploys Are Often Toppers,
They Don't 'Cement' Friendship With Coppers.

THE BROONS

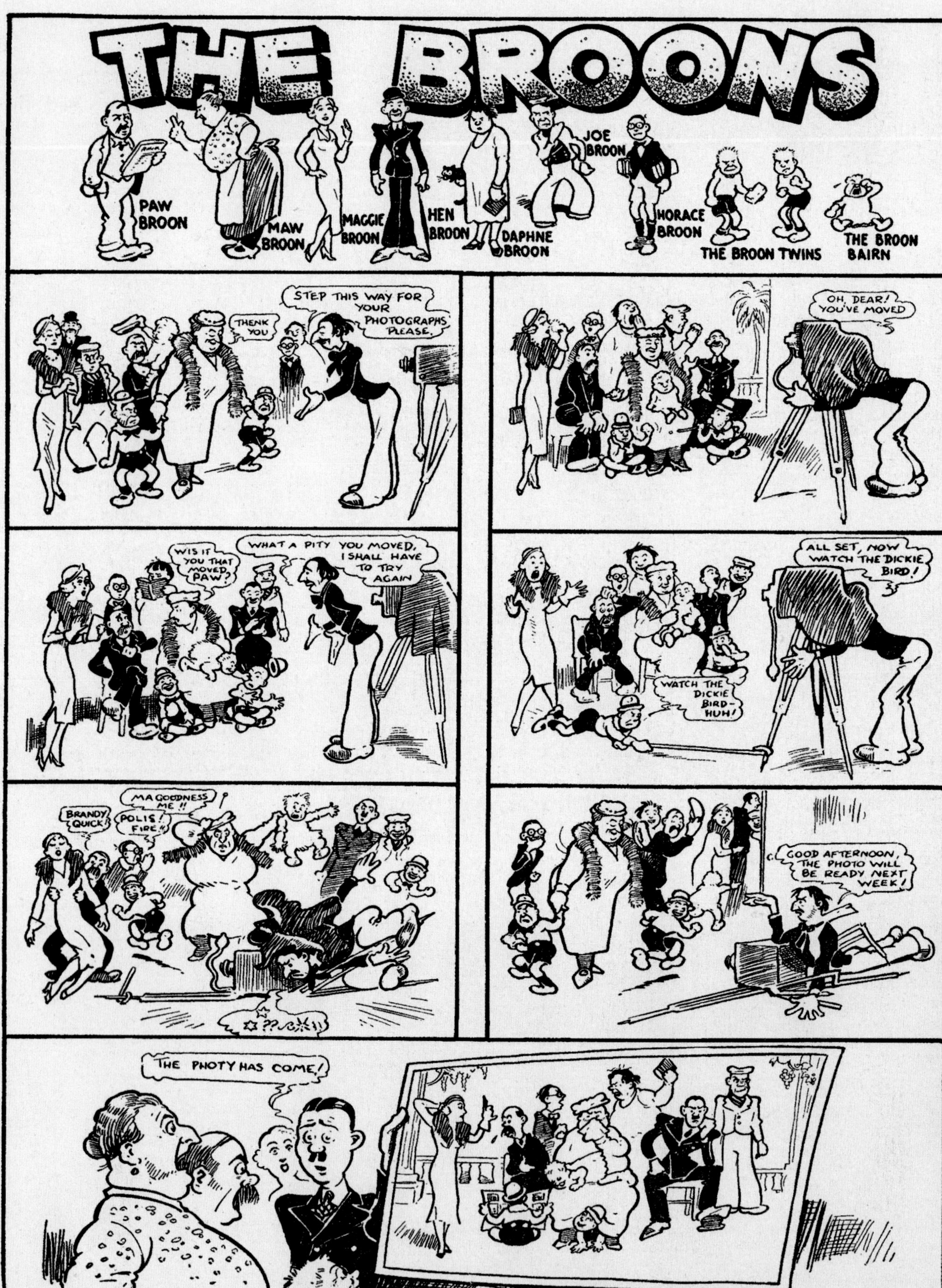

PAW BROON
MAW BROON
MAGGIE BROON
HEN BROON
DAPHNE BROON
JOE BROON
HORACE BROON
THE BROON TWINS
THE BROON BAIRN
STEP THIS WAY FOR YOUR PHOTOGRAPHS PLEASE.
THENK YOU
OH, DEAR! YOU'VE MOVED
WIS IT YOU THAT MOVED PAW?
WHAT A PITY YOU MOVED, I SHALL HAVE TO TRY AGAIN
ALL SET, NOW WATCH THE DICKIE BIRD!
WATCH THE DICKIE BIRD-HUH!
BRANDY QUICK!
MA GOODNESS ME !!
POLIS! FIRE!
??
GOOD AFTERNOON, THE PHOTO WILL BE READY NEXT WEEK!
THE PHOTY HAS COME!

There's A "Cat-And-Dog-Fight" At The Broons, But Paw Collects The Winnings.

Granpaw Is Eighty-Eight Years Young;
They'll Hae Him Shot, If He's No' Hung.

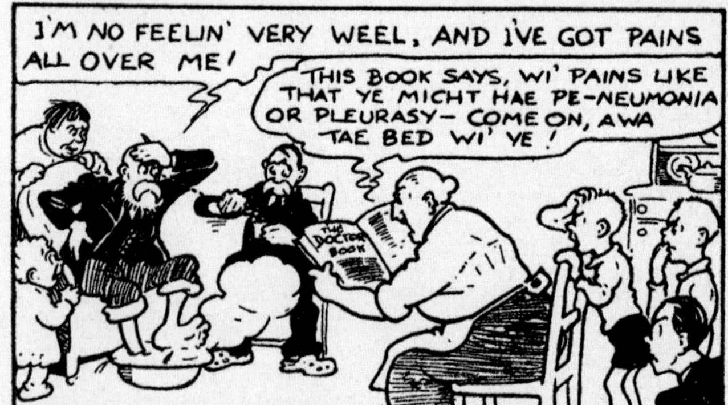

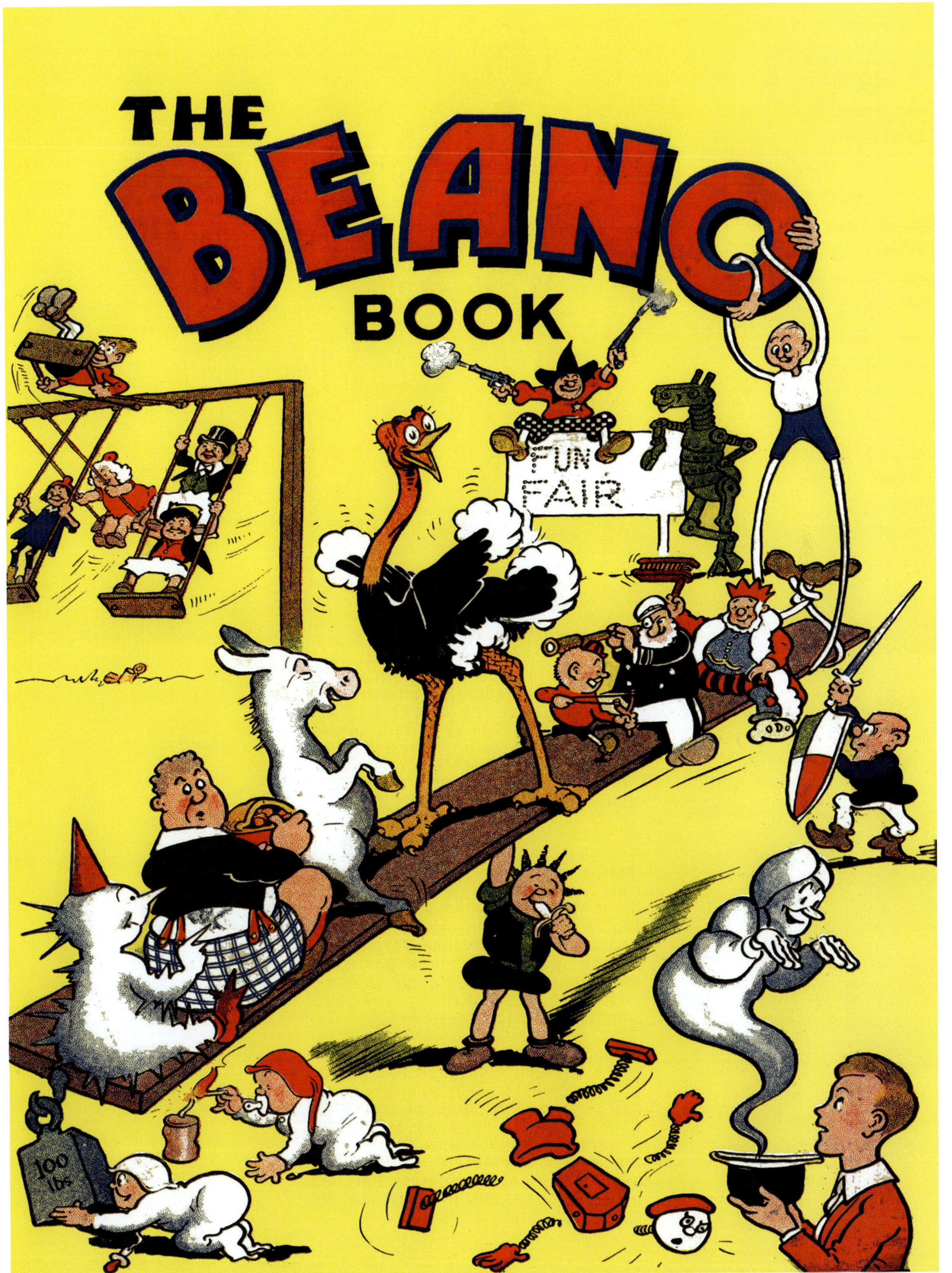
THE BEANO BOOK
FUN FAIR
100 lbs

DESPERATE DAN

Smashing onto the scene in 1937 was a certain daring desperado by the name of Desperate Dan. After his stellar work on The Broons and Oor Wullie in 1936, Dudley D Watkins was approached by editor, Albert Barnes, to draw the character for the very first issue of The Dandy. It's even said that Watkins modelled Dan's infamous barrel chin on Barnes' own square jaw.

Originally just a half page, Watkins' humour shone immediately, as the heavy cowboy's newly-bought horse buckled under Dan's weight. Proclaiming he had been ripped off, Dan returned to the vendor for revenge for selling him a dud horse. But, when the strongman swung a punch — he missed, instead striking the tree which fell to squish the vendor.

From this point onwards, the character was a resounding success, and Dudley D Watkins went from gradually drawing half pages to two-thirds of a page, to a full page, double-page strips and onwards. There was a lot in store for the cow-poke's future as Watkins' humble half-page Desperate Dan has gone on to be one of the most famous Dandy characters in history.

I WANT A HORSE! AND IT'S GOTTA BE TOUGH BECAUSE I'M DESPERATE DAN!
THE HORSE DEALER OF BAD MAN'S GULCH —
THIS IS A REAL TOUGH HORSE MISTER!
IT'D BETTER BE!
BAD MAN'S GULCH 1 MILE
BAD MAN'S GULCH ½ MILE
SELL ME A DUD HORSE WOULD YOU?
AW GEE, DAN! YOU WOULDN'T BEAT ME UP WOULD YOU?
WHOOF
OH WELL! I GOT HIM ANYWAY!
GOSH! SEEING THESE KIDS PLAYING WITH BOWS AND ARROWS REMINDS ME OF THE FUN I USED TO HAVE WITH THEM MYSELF WHEN I WAS A KID!
WOULDN'T YOU LIKE TO BE YOUNG AGAIN, DAN?
I GUESS I'LL MAKE ME A BOW AND ARROW — ONLY IT'LL HAVE TO BE PLENTY TOUGH! THIS TREE'LL DO FOR A BOW!
TUG
— AND A FEW TELEPHONE POLES FOR ARROWS!
ROOTS →
SNAP
DAN'S BRACES
AH! THERE'S A BIRD! I'LL SEE IF I CAN HIT IT!
CRASH
WHOOPEE! A BULL'S EYE!
JUMPING CATS! I'VE SHOT DOWN AN AEROPLANE!
YOU BIG GOOF! THIS IS THE MAIL PLANE, AND NOW THE MAIL WON'T GO THROUGH!
LATER
SHE'S ALL FIXED NOW, DAN, EXCEPT THAT SHE ISN'T STRONG ENOUGH TO RISE OFF THE GROUND!
JUST YOU LEAVE THAT TO ME, BUDDY!
ARE YOU ALL SET, PAL?
SURE, LET HER GO, DAN!
HA! THAT'S DONE THE TRICK! I KNEW I WAS A GOOD BOWMAN!
SO LONG, DANNY BOY!

HUH! NO PESKY FLY CAN BUZZ ROUND DESPERATE DAN AND GET AWAY WITH IT!
Z-Z-Z
I'LL STOP YOUR TRICKS!
Z-Z-Z
AH! - THERE IT IS, ON THE WALL! Z-Z-Z
SO YOU'D TRICK ME, WOULD YOU? YOU'RE ON THIS WALL NOW!
BUMP
WOW! - IT'S STUCK IN MY TREACLE PUDDING, NOW - HA-HA!!
OH, WELL, I GOT YOU THAT TIME ANYWAY!
WAITER! - WAITER! - I WANT MY HASH!
- AND I WANT IT QUICK, BECAUSE I'M DESPERATE DAN!
CONK
KITCHEN
I'LL GIVE HIM HASH!!
I'LL JUST FLAVOUR HIS HASH WITH A FEW BULLETS!
BULLETS
HASH
- SOME MOULDY OLD FEATHERS OFF THAT HEN THAT DIED!
HASH
LAST BUT NOT LEAST - HALF A PINT OF POISON
HASH
YOUR HASH, SIR!
AND IT'S ABOUT TIME TOO!
SWOON
HERE'S A DOLLAR FOR YOU, THAT'S THE BEST HASH I'VE EVER HAD!

FIRE STATION
I'LL HAVE A SNOOZE IN HERE TILL THE RAIN STOPS.
ALL ABOARD BOYS! THERE'S A BIG FIRE DOWN THE ROAD!
FIRE BELL
CLANG CLANG
GOSH! WHAT'S HOLDING US BACK? THE WHEELS ARE WHIZZING ROUND BUT WE'RE NOT MOVING AN INCH!
LOOK! IT'S DESPERATE DAN WHO'S KEEPING US FROM MOVING — WAKE HIM UP!
SNORE
THIS OUGHT TO WAKEN HIM!
SMASH
SKID
HEY, DAN! THERE'S A FIRE, AND YOU'RE HOLDING THE ENGINE BACK!
YAWN
GOSH! I FORGOT TO PUT ON THE BRAKES, AND THE ENGINE'S RUNNING AWAY!!
SORRY BOYS!
YAWN
CRASH
THE ENGINE'S SMASHED TO PIECES! WHAT'LL WE DO NOW?
DON'T WORRY, BOYS, SHOW ME THIS FIRE — I'LL FIX IT FOR YOU!
JUST WATCH THIS!
BLOW
HOLY SMOKE! DAN'S BLOWN THE FIRE OUT!!
PRIDE
FERRY BOAT
HOI! COME BACK! I WANT TO CROSS THE RIVER!
FERRY
HUH! THEY'RE PAYING NO ATTENTION, ALL RIGHT! I'LL LASSO THE MAST AND DRAG THEM BACK!
FERRY
GOSH! I'VE PULLED THE MAST RIGHT OFF!
WOW
HEY
FERRY
I'LL GET THE BOAT BY THE RUDDER THIS TIME!
OH HELP! I'VE MISSED AGAIN!
HELP
OH WELL, I'LL JUST HAVE TO JUMP FOR IT!
CORKS! WHAT A JUMP! DAN'S GONE RIGHT THROUGH THE BOAT!
FERRY
60 MILES AN HOUR
I'LL JUST HAVE TO SWIM ACROSS
FERRY
WELL, WHY ARE YOU ALL LOOKING SO GLOOMY, I GOT YOU ACROSS, DIDN'T I?
YOU BLINKING ASS! YOU'VE TAKEN US BACK TO WHERE WE CAME FROM!!
FERRY

LORD SNOOTY

Lord Snooty, or Lord Marmaduke of Bunkerton to refer to him by his full title, appeared in the first issue of Beano in 1938. The strip was originally dubbed Lord Snooty and his Pals, and boasted a full cast of Snooty's chums, including Skinny Lizzie, Hairpin Huggins, and good old Gertie the Goat, all drawn by none other than Dudley D Watkins.

But the Earl often traverses the class divide, being upper class but playing a double life with his poor, working-class friends. Although the young master had numerous butlers, servants, and a fancy manor house, the scamp often climbed over the garden wall disguised as a street urchin to play with his real pals from Ash Can Alley.

In his very first issue, it's Lord Snooty's birthday and, not satisfied with his presents, he pays a visit to his friends who have built him a cart pulled along by Gertie — only his insufferable upper-class acquaintances have a similar idea, leading to a tremendous crash. Peppered with classic Dudley D Watkins' humour, from the butler's popping button in panel three to the gasping horse in panel ten, the strip was a hit and Watkins continued to illustrate it regularly until April 1968.

LORD SNOOTY AND HIS PALS
LORD MARMADUKE— "SNOOTY" TO YOU!
ROSIE.
HAIRPIN HUGGINS.
SKINNY LIZZIE.
SCRAPPER SMITH.
"HAPPY" HUTTON.
GERTIE THE GOAT

MANY HAPPY RETURNS OF THE DAY, YOUR LORDSHIP!
GOOD MORNING, AUNT!
GOOD MORNING, MARMADUKE. LOOK AT ALL THE NICE BIRTHDAY GIFTS YOUR FRIENDS HAVE SENT YOU!
WHAT'S MORE, ALGERNON, PERCIVAL AND VERNON TOOTLE ARE ON THEIR WAY HERE NOW WITH A PRESENT OF A DOG-CART FOR YOU!
H—M!
NOW, GO UPSTAIRS AND WASH. YOU MUST BE VERY NICE TO THE LITTLE BOYS WHEN THEY COME!
HUH! THOSE THREE TOOTLE GUYS GIVE ME A PAIN IN THE NECK! I'LL DODGE 'EM BY SNEAKING DOWN THE DRAIN-PIPE!
I'LL CHANGE INTO MY DISGUISE AND GO TO MEET MY REAL PALS DOWN IN ASH-CAN ALLEY!
GEE! I'M GOING TO SPEND A REAL HAPPY BIRTHDAY WITH MY PALS!
HI! FELLERS!
HAPPY BIRTHDAY, SNOOTY! LOOK WHAT WE'VE GOT FOR YOUR BIRTHDAY PRESENT!
GEE! THIS IS THE BEST BIRTHDAY PRESENT I'VE EVER HAD!
AW SHUCKS
CORKS! IT'S ALGY, PERCY AND VERNON!
WOOF
GASP
THEY DIDN'T KNOW ME IN THESE OLD CLOTHES! GOSH! WHAT A LARK IT'LL BE WHEN THEY BRING HOME THAT DOG-CART FOR ME!
CHEERIO, GANG! I'M GOING BACK TO CHANGE INTO MY ETON SUIT—KEEP THE CART FOR ME!
S'LONG SNOOTY!
GOOD MORNING, YOUR LORDSHIP,—WE HAVE—ER—A BIRTHDAY GIFT FOR YOU OUTSIDE, THOUGH WE HAVE HAD AN ACCIDENT ON THE WAY HERE!
THOUGHT, GEE! IF THEY ONLY KNEW IT WAS ME WHO SMASHED IT UP!
WHAT! YOU CALL THAT A BIRTHDAY PRESENT? HOW DARE YOU INSULT THE EARL OF BUNKERTON WITH A WRECK LIKE THAT! TAKE THAT AWFUL THING AWAY!!

LORD SNOOTY
AND
HIS PALS
LORD MARMADUKE— "SNOOTY" TO YOU!
ROSIE.
HAIRPIN HUGGINS.
SKINNY LIZZIE.
SCRAPPER SMITH.
"HAPPY" HUTTON.
GERTIE THE GOAT

I'LL GO DOWN TO ASH-CAN ALLEY AND MEET THE GANG COMING OUT OF SCHOOL!

WAKE UP, YOU LAZY LITTLE BRATS. KNEES BEND, ARMS SIDEWAYS STRETCH, I'LL MAKE YOU WORK AS YOU'VE NEVER WORKED BEFORE!
GOSH! THAT MUST BE BLINKER, THE GANG'S NEW GYM INSTRUCTOR. WHAT A BRUTE HE IS!
SMACK
ASH-CAN COUNCIL SCHOOL

AFTER SCHOOL.
PHEW! EVERY DAY OLD BLINKER HALF KILLS US WITH HIS GYM LESSON!
LEAVE THIS TO ME! I'LL FIX THE CAD!

CAN I HAVE AN INSTRUCTOR TO GIVE ME GYMS, AUNT MILDRED?
CERTAINLY, LORD MARMADUKE, I SHALL ENGAGE THE FAMOUS SERGEANT MAJOR BELLOWS!

LEFT-RIGHT! LEFT-RIGHT! LEFT-RIGHT! FASTER PLEASE, YOUR LORDSHIP!
I WOW! NOW KNOW WHAT THE GANG HAVE TO SUFFER!

I ENJOYED GYMS VERY MUCH, AUNTIE, IN FACT I'D LIKE TO STAGE A GYM CONTEST IN THE TOWN HALL!
A SPLENDID IDEA, MY DEAR BOY!

GRAND ENDURANCE CONTEST FOR GYMNASTS STARTS AT 7 O'CLOCK IN TOWN HALL TO-NIGHT FIRST PRIZE— A SOLID SILVER CUP!
I'LL BET THIS STUNT OF MINE FOOLS YOUR GYM TEACHER, LADS!

TOWN HALL
PASS ON PLEASE, SERGEANT MAJOR, AND THE BEST OF LUCK TO YOU. —NEXT PLEASE!
GEE! THERE'S BLINKER, OUR GYM TEACHER ENTERING!

BEND, STRETCH! BEND, STRETCH! FASTER PLEASE, GENTLEMEN!

TOUCH YOUR TOES—HOLLOW YOUR BACKS!
HO! HO! EVERYBODY'S DROPPED OUT EXCEPT BLINKER AND THE SERGEANT MAJOR. I'LL GIVE THEM A DOSE OF THEIR OWN MEDICINE!

—KNEES BEND! KNEES STRETCH! LEG FLINGING EXERCISE, COMMENCE! GOSH! IT'S TWELVE O'CLOCK AND THEY'RE BOTH DEAD BEAT!
I'LL BEAT YOU— GASP— YET— GASP!
OH NO— GASP— YOU WON'T!

HALF AN HOUR LATER.
I DECLARE THE CONTEST A DRAW, AND AS BOTH GENTLEMEN DESERVE TO WIN, THERE IS ONLY ONE FAIR THING WE CAN DO WITH THE PRIZE!
SNORE
SNORE

—CUT THE CUP IN TWO AND GIVE EACH OF THEM A HALF OF IT!

HOSPITAL
HO! HO! BLINKER HAS NEARLY KILLED HIMSELF TO WIN THE CUP. IT'LL BE WEEKS BEFORE HE'LL BE BACK AT SCHOOL TO BOTHER US!
OOH! I'LL NEVER BE THE SAME AGAIN!
WELL, I WON HALF THE CUP, ANYWAY!

LORD MARMADUKE—
"SNOOTY" TO YOU!
ROSIE.
HAIRPIN HUGGINS.
SKINNY LIZZIE.
SCRAPPER SMITH.
"HAPPY" HUTTON.
GERTIE THE GOAT
LORD SNOOTY AND HIS PALS

WE ARE HAVING A FANCY DRESS PARTY, TOMORROW, MARMADUKE! THESE ARE THE INVITATION CARDS. INVITE ALL YOUR NICEST LITTLE FRIENDS!
WHAT A CHANCE TO INVITE MY REAL PALS TO THE PARTY!
NOW I'M DISGUISED, I'LL BUZZ DOWN TO ASH-CAN ALLEY TO MEET THE GANG!
YOU'RE ALL COMING TO OUR FANCY DRESS PARTY, SO YOU'LL NEED SWANKY NAMES ON YOUR INVITATION CARDS. AUNT WONT KNOW THE DIFFERENCE!
GOSH! WHAT A SWELL NAME SNOOTY'S GIVEN ME. LORD HUBERT HUTTON!
LOOK OUT, LADS! DUGAN THE COP'S WATCHING US!
I'M GOING AS THE HONOURABLE ELIZABETH MONTMORENCY!

NEXT NIGHT AT THE PARTY
LADIES AND GENTLEMEN— LITTLE LORD HUBERT HUTTON AND PARTY!
GOODNESS! AREN'T THOSE CHILDREN WELL DISGUISED? THEY SIMPLY LOOK LIKE A GANG OF REAL STREET KIDS!— TOO PERFECTLY MARVELLOUS!
ASH-CAN ALLEY GANG
BOW
WELCOME TO OUR HUMBLE PARTY, YOUR LADYSHIP! (WHISPER→) YOU ARE DOING FINE!
HA-HA-HA!! LOOK AT THE HONOURABLE HAIRPIN HUGGINS COOLING HIS TEA WITH HIS CAP!
OH, YES, HE KNOWS HOW TO ACT THE PART OF A TOUGH EGG!

GOSH! THERE'S SO MANY SUITS OF ARMOUR AND FOLKS IN FANCY COSTUMES IN THIS 'OUSE THAT I DON'T KNOW WHICH IS REAL AND WHICH IS NOT!
WELL, TRY HITTING ONE OF 'EM, WIV AN AXE!
GOSH! THATS A REAL MAN ANYWAY.
WOW! IT'S THE KIDS FROM ASH-CAN ALLEY!
I'LL SAY IT IS! IT'S OLD DUGAN THE COP!
YOU'VE NO BUSINESS BEING HERE. I'LL TELL HER LADYSHIP WHO YOU ARE!
CORKS! THIS WILL LAND SNOOTY IN THE SOUP!
LET'S SLIDE DOWN THE BANNISTERS!

GOSH! WE'RE IN FOR IT, IF THE BOBBY TELLS WHO WE ARE!
SLIDE
LOOK AT THOSE JEWELS IN THAT GUY'S HELMET! HE MUST BE A JEWEL THIEF.— THE VERY MAN THE INSPECTOR SENT ME HERE TO WATCH FOR!
COME ON, LAD, I'VE GOT YOU AND THE JEWELS TOO!
SEEING YOU'VE HELPED ME TO GET THIS JEWEL THIEF, I WONT TELL LORD MARMADUKE'S AUNT ABOUT YOU!
BUMP

THE JUDGES HAVE CHOSEN YOUR FANCY DRESS AS THE BEST OF THE EVENING, I AM DELIGHTED TO HAND YOU THE PRIZE!
GEE! THIS IS THE BEST MEAL I'VE HAD ALL NIGHT!
IS THAT TEN POUND NOTES I SEE? OH, WE'LL BE ABLE TO HAVE A GRAND TIME WITH THAT!
THANK YOU FOR A VERY PLEASANT EVENING, LORD HUBERT!

LORD SNOOTY AND HIS PALS
LORD MARMADUKE— "SNOOTY" TO YOU!
ROSIE.
HAIRPIN HUGGINS.
SKINNY LIZZIE.
SCRAPPER SMITH.
"HAPPY" HUTTON.
GERTIE THE GOAT.

KEEP YOUR DISTANCE IF YOU PLEASE, LADY MATILDA. ALL THE SERVANTS HAVE CAUGHT MUMPS, AND IT WILL BE IMPOSSIBLE FOR THEM TO SERVE AT YOUR CHARITY BANQUET TONIGHT!
WHAT A PITY, AND I'VE INVITED CROWDS OF POOR PEOPLE UP TO THE CASTLE TONIGHT!

GOLLY, WE CAN'T PUT THE BANQUET OFF. I'LL HAVE TO GO DOWN AND GET THE ASH-CAN ALLEY GANG TO HELP ME!
KEEP BACK, LORD MARMADUKE, OR YOU'LL GET THEM TOO!

ALL MY SERVANTS ARE ILL, SO THE OLD FOLKS WON'T GET THIS FREE FEED UNLESS WE CAN GET NEW ONES, QUICK!
GREAT FREE BANQUET FOR OLD-AGE PENSIONERS AT BUNKERTON CASTLE TONIGHT. FOR ADMISSION TICKET, APPLY TO LADY MATILDA OR LORD MARMADUKE BUNKERTON.
HEY SNITCHY! DON'T LET THAT MOUSE OF YOURS BITE MY CAT!
WHAT A SHAME!

OH BOY! THESE JUGGLERS ARE GOOD!

YOU CAN'T DO THAT THAT THERE. COME ALONG TO THE COP SHOP!
GOSH! THOSE JUGGLERS HAVE GIVEN ME AN IDEA. I'LL GET THEM OUT OF JAIL!

INSPECTOR MONTGOMERY, I DEMAND YOU TO SET THOSE THREE MEN FREE! I NEED THEIR HELP!
CERTAINLY, LORD MARMADUKE!
THUMP
PLEASE DO NOT STICK YOUR CHEWING GUM HERE
BEANO

JAIL
THANKS, PAL! YOU SAVED OUR BACON!
THAT'S O.K., BOYS. NOW I WANT YOU TO DO ME A FAVOUR!

LOOK, AUNTIE, THOSE THREE CHAPS WILL SERVE THE TABLES AT THE BANQUET TONIGHT!
BUT IT'S FAR TOO BIG A TASK FOR ONLY THREE MEN!

FIRE AHEAD, BOYS! THEY'RE WAITING FOR YOU!

FASTER, ALBERT, PLEASE!
KITCHEN
LOOK, SNITCH, I CAN DO IT!
SO CAN I—OW!

TURKEY
GRAVY

THIS IS BETTER THAN THE MOVIES!

THREE CHEERS FOR LORD SNOOTY
HIP-HIP-HOORAY!

LORD SNOOTY AND HIS PALS
LORD MARMADUKE— "SNOOTY" TO YOU!
ROSIE.
HAIRPIN HUGGINS.
SKINNY LIZZIE.
SCRAPPER SMITH.
"HAPPY" HUTTON.
GERTIE THE GOAT

EXCUSE ME, SIR, BUT I'VE COME TO ASK YOUR PERMISSION TO TEACH LORD SNOOTY AND HIS PALS TO DO THE HIGHLAND SWORD DANCE!
WHY, CERTAINLY, SERGEANT MAC DUFF. LORD SNOOTY'S AUNT HAS BEEN KIND ENOUGH TO BILLET US IN THE CASTLE AND THAT'S THE LEAST WE CAN DO.
SIGN ME ON, SIR—FOR THE INFANT-RY!
HEADQUARTERS OF 1st HIGHLAND REGIMENT

THE CAMPBELLS ARE COMING
G-GOLLY! THIS IS TERRIBLE! WE NEVER THOUGHT MAC DUFF WOULD PLAY AT THIS SPEED!
GEE! WE'VE BEEN DANCING FOR HOURS AND MAC DUFF WON'T LET US STOP!
I'M NEARLY DROPPING!

BE HERE AGAIN AT SIX O'CLOCK TOMORROW MORNING, YOU KIDS AND NO SNEAKING OFF!
THEY'RE TIRED OUT! WE'LL HAVE TO CARRY THEM OFF!
Z-Z
GASP
PHEW! HAVE THIS CAKE, SNITCHY!
NO THANKS! WHAT I NEED IS THREE DAYS IN BED!
HOME, JAMES, AND DON'T SPARE THE HORSES!
GURR! WHAT LIFE!

YES, THANK YOU, SNOOTY, WE'RE HAVING A FINE TIME. THERE'S ONLY ONE THING WRONG—WE CAN'T GET ANY EXERCISE!
WELL, COLONEL, WHY DON'T YOU TAKE UP HIGHLAND DANCING AND GET SERGEANT MAC DUFF TO PLAY FOR YOU?
I THINK THAT'S A SPLENDID IDEA, COLONEL!

LISTEN, GANG! I'VE GOT AN IDEA TO GET OUR OWN BACK ON THAT NASTY BULLY, MAC DUFF, BUT FIRST WE'VE GOT TO GET SOME LAUGHING GAS FROM THE DENTISTS!
O.K. SNITCHY'LL HELP US, WON'T YOU, SNITCH?
GR-R-R
GO ON, SNITCHY, YOU'RE ONLY A KID YET!

OUR PAL'S GOT TOOTHACHE, MR DENTIST, WILL YOU FIX HIM?
WHY, SURE! COME IN, MY LITTLE MAN!
MR PULLEM, DENTIST
HUH, THE BIG BOZO!

GOODNESS! HOW CAN HE HAVE TOOTHACHE? HE HASN'T ANY TEETH!
HOWL YELL OUCH! MURDER!!
HOWL YELL OUCH MURDER!!
G-GOSH! I'D RATHER HAVE TOOTHACHE THAN SUFFER THAT, I'M OFF!
GEE! ME TOO!
KNOCK KNOCK

GOODNESS! THAT LITTLE WRETCH HAS SCARED ALL OF MY PATIENTS AWAY!
THEY WENT THAT WAY, AFTER THEM, SIR, AND YOU'LL CATCH 'EM!
MR PULLEM DENTIST

IN YOU COME, LADS! OLD PULLEM'S BUSY TRYING TO GET BACK HIS PATIENTS!
HURRY, SNOOTY! THERE'S THE LAUGHING GAS. WE JUST WANT TO BORROW IT!
BOY! AM I GLAD TO SEE YOU!
LAUGHING GAS

YES, SIR! I'LL BE GLAD TO PLAY THE BAGPIPES WHILE YOU AND THE OTHER OFFICERS DO THE SWORD DANCE!
NOW FOR IT, GANG! FILL MAC DUFF'S BAGPIPES FULL OF LAUGHING GAS!
LAUGHING GAS
VERY WELL, MACDUFF, GO AHEAD!
NEXT MORNING

DRONE GROAN SQUEAK
HAR! HAR! HAR! OW! I CANT STOP LAUGHING! HA! HA! HA!
WHAT!!— MACDUFF LAUGHING AT HIS SUPERIOR OFFICERS?— HE'LL GET A TASTE OF JAIL FOR THIS!
WHOOPEE! LOOK AT WHAT THE LAUGHING GAS HAS DONE TO MAC DUFF!

GEE! AIN'T OUR MUSIC SWEET!
SOUTH OF THE BORDER
PLAY UP, SNOOTY, MAC DUFF LIKES YOUR PLAYING!
CELLS
THAT'LL TEACH YOU NOT TO BULLY US, MACDUFF!
LOOK AT SNITCHY AND SNATCHY, THE SILLY CHUMPS THINK THEY'RE HELPING!

LORD MARMADUKE— "SNOOTY" TO YOU!
ROSIE.
HAIRPIN HUGGINS.
SKINNY LIZZIE.
SCRAPPER SMITH.
"HAPPY" HUTTON.
GERTIE THE GOAT
LORD SNOOTY AND HIS PALS

HULLO COOK! THAT'S A FINE LOT OF GRUB YOU'VE GOT FOR DINNER!
YES, LORD MARMADUKE.
GOSH! I WISH I COULD GET MY ASH-CAN ALLEY PALS UP TO THE CASTLE FOR DINNER!
I'VE GOT AN IDEA! I'LL CHANGE INTO MY DISGUISE!
I'LL WRAP UP MY ETON SUIT IN THIS BROWN PAPER, AND TAKE IT WITH ME. I'LL BE DOWN TO ASH-CAN ALLEY IN TWO TICKS!
HI! GANG! I'VE GOT A SWELL IDEA TO MAKE MY AUNT GIVE YOU DINNER UP AT THE CASTLE TODAY. NOW LISTEN—!
I'M NOT GOING BACK TO THE CASTLE ALL AFTERNOON!
DINNER TIME
ALBERT, HAVE YOU SEEN LORD MARMADUKE? DINNER IS SERVED!
NO, YOUR LADYSHIP!
THEN HAVE THE FOOTMEN SEARCH THE GROUNDS, AND YOU GO INTO THE ROAD TO SEE IF HE CAN BE FOUND!
BOW
20 MINUTES LATER
OH! YOUR LADYSHIP! WE'VE SEARCHED EVERYWHERE, AND THERE'S NOT A SIGN OF HIS LORDSHIP!—MAYBE HE'S LOST OR HAS BEEN KIDNAPPED!!
SCREAM
I'LL HAVE TO GO AND SEARCH FOR MARMADUKE MYSELF! I'LL ASK THIS YOUNG STREET URCHIN. HE MAY BE ABLE TO HELP ME.
HERE'S AUNTY LOOKING FOR ME, JUST AS I EXPECTED. SHE'LL NEVER RECOGNISE ME IN THESE CLOTHES!
I HAVE LOST LORD MARMADUKE, MY LITTLE NEPHEW, HAVE YOU SEEN HIM?
IS THAT THE POSH LITTLE GINK WOT LIVES IN THE CASTLE? CRIPES! I THINK I KNOW WHERE HE IS!
HEY, GANG! COME AND HELP US TO FIND LORD MARMADUKE!
OH SURE!
YES! I THINK HE'S OVER HERE SOMEWHERE!
I'LL DODGE BEHIND THIS HEDGE AND CHANGE INTO MY POSH CLOTHES!
NOW I'M ALL SET, I'LL SIGNAL THE GANG!
WHISTLE
HERE'S LORD MARMADUKE, MISSUS! WE TOLD YOU WE'D FIND HIM!
THE POOR BOY MUST BE ILL!
BRING HIM INTO THE CASTLE QUICKLY!
WHERE AM I? OH! I MUST HAVE FAINTED!
THESE CHILDREN FOUND YOU AND BROUGHT YOU HOME!
HELP YOURSELVES NOW, CHILDREN! THIS DINNER IS IN YOUR HONOUR FOR FINDING MY DEAR LITTLE MARMADUKE!
WELL, I CERTAINLY GOT MY PALS UP TO THE HOUSE FOR A GOOD FEED! AND DID THEY ENJOY IT?— YOU'RE TELLING ME!

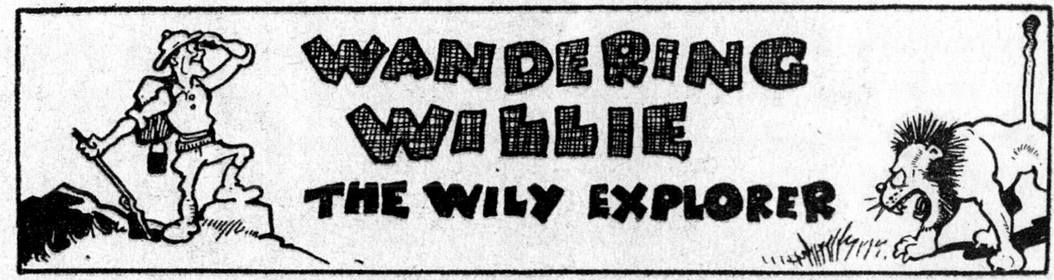

WANDERING
WILLIE
THE WILY EXPLORER

COME ON — NICE PUSSY.

THUD
BONK

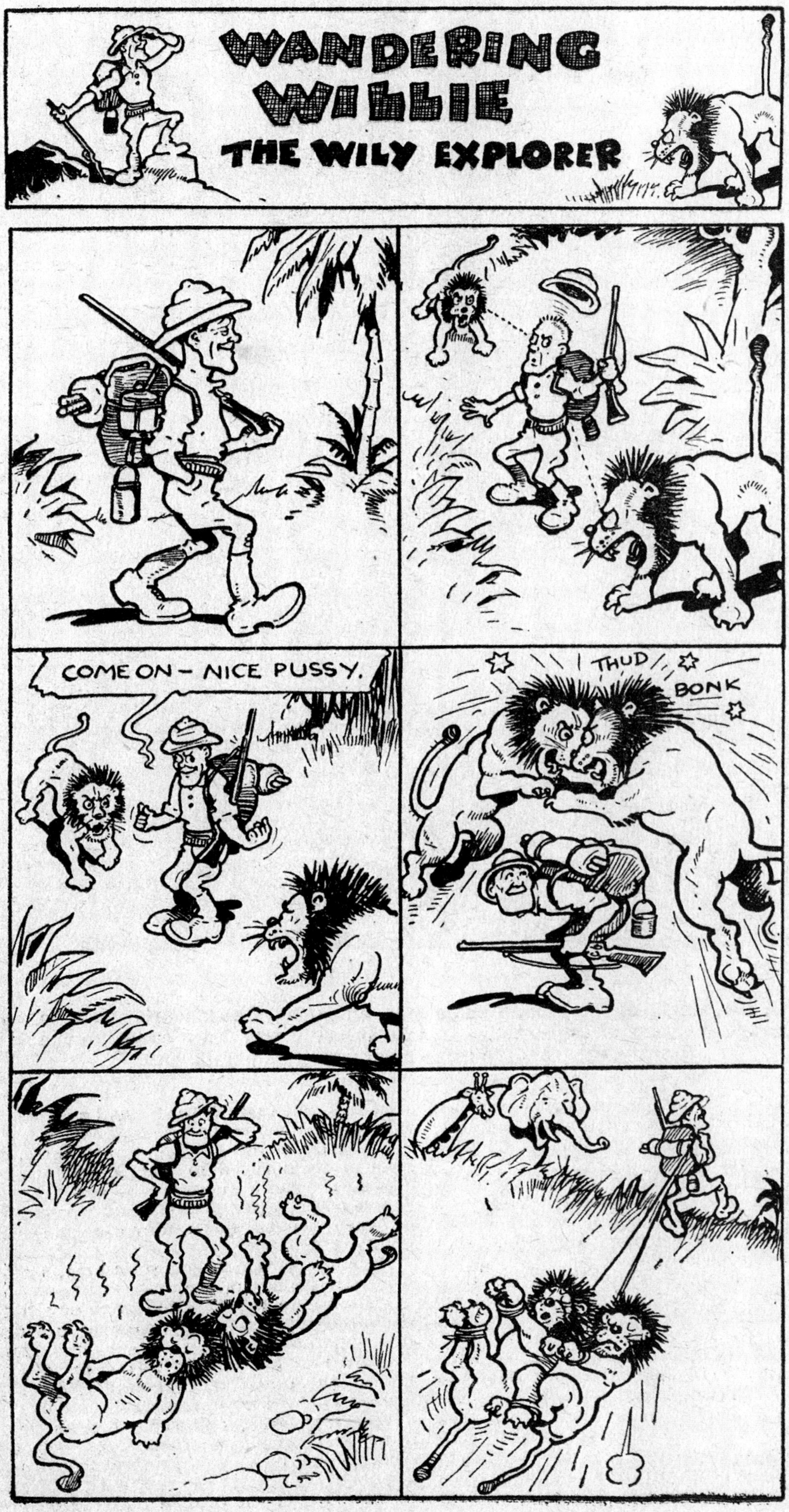

WANDERING
WILLIE
THE WILY EXPLORER
POP
HAH! — WATER!
BLOW
RED PEPPER
RED PEPPER
AH-TISH-OO
SNEEZE —
ASH-ER!!
A-A-A-

Willie " sells " the crocs " the dummy!"

WANDERING WILLIE
THE WILY EXPLORER

GEE! HOW'M I GOING TO GET A CROSS THIS RIVER WITH ALL THESE CROCODILES IN IT?
IDEA
THANKS!

Panel 1:

Panel 2:

Panel 3:

Panel 4:

Panel 5:

Panel 6:

PERCY VERE
AND HIS TRYING TRICKS
MAGIC ?

I'M GOING TO PLAY A TRICK ON MY GUESTS WHEN THEY DRINK THE NEW YEAR IN WITH GINGER WINE

WATCH ME TURN THE GINGER WINE INTO VINEGAR, WE'LL HAVE THE WINE OURSELVES

USE THIS EMPTY DECANTER
A GOOD JOKE PERCY!

HEY! SWITCH THAT LIGHT ON!

I'VE GOT MINE OUT OF THE OTHER DECANTER

PERCY'S PLAYED A TRICK ON HIMSELF!

PERCY VERE
AND HIS TRYING TRICKS
MAGIC ?

LEND ME YOUR BAT BOYS, AND I'LL SHOW YOU A CONJURING TRICK
PUT THE BAT UNDER MY COAT - SO!
FEEL THIS - THE BAT IS REALLY UNDER THE COAT, ISNT IT?
YES
TAKE AWAY THE COAT AND SEE WHAT HAS HAPPENED, HA-HA!
HOWL
RAGE
BREAK OUR BAT, WOULD YOU?
GURGLE - GURGLE - I'VE NOT REALLY BROKEN IT - UGH!
I'LL NEVER TRY ANY TRICKS ON THOSE BOYS AGAIN

SMARTY GRANDPA

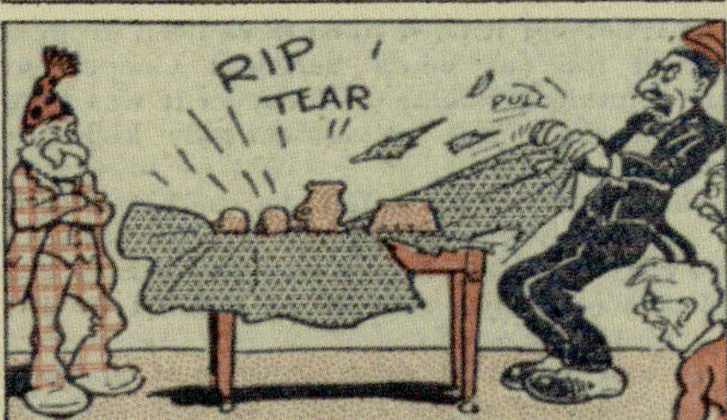

SMARTY GRANDPA

SMARTY GRANDPA

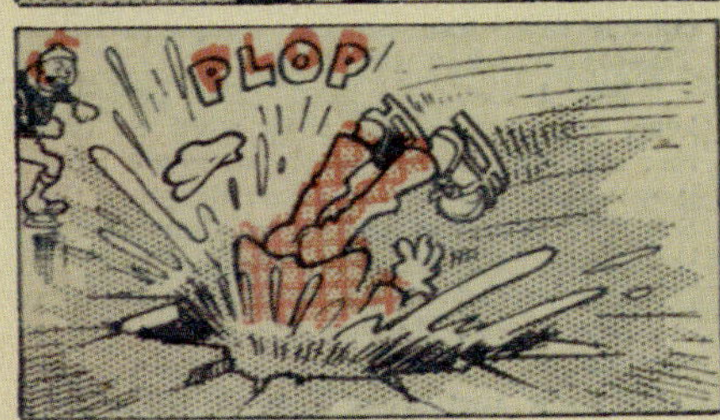

1940s

During World War Two, Watkins' work was judged to be so valuable to public morale that he was excluded from military service and instead became a War Reserve Constable in Kincardine, which allowed him to continue his work for the publisher in Dundee. Here he met PC Sandy Marnoch who may have inspired Oor Wullie's local bobby, PC Murdoch.

On the 1st January, 1944, the time-travelling schoolboy Jimmy and his Magic Patch debuted in Beano, showcasing Watkins' realism. A couple of years later, he started signing his work — one of only two artists at DC Thomson to do so, the other being Allan Morley who drew numerous strips for Beano and The Dandy, including Keyhole Kate. During this era he bought his home, Winsterley, in Broughty Ferry. Here, Biffo the Bear was born and graced Beano's front cover.

JIMMY
AND HIS MAGIC PATCH

His longest-running adventure strip, Jimmy and his Magic Patch, was drawn by Watkins from issue No.222 of Beano in 1944 until 1949. Rendered in a more realistic art style than Watkins' other humour strips, Jimmy was known for having more of a picture book format, similar to his earlier strips — The Adventures of Tom Thumb and Dick Whittington and his Cat.

A schoolchild's daydream thrill, Jimmy's adventures centred on his magical time-travelling trouser patch (a gift given to him by an old lady whose cat he saved, unfortunately splitting his trousers in the process). Over the years, Jimmy's adventures took him through the centuries, meeting historical figures like Robert the Bruce and Alfred the Great, as well as legends like Robin Hood and Sinbad the Sailor.

JIMMY AND HIS MAGIC PATCH

1—It was Saturday afternoon and Jimmy Watson, with his home-made pirate outfit, walked down to the pond near the village. It was as he reached it that he noticed two of his pals striding towards him. "Hi, chums!" he yelled, waving his wooden sword. "Let's get aboard our raft and play pirates again." One of the lads waved a derisive hand. "Bah!" he said. "We're going to the pictures to see a real pirate picture!"

2—Jimmy's face fell as they walked away and left him at the edge of the pond. "If only I had enough money to go to the pictures," he muttered. "I wish I could see real pirates, too." Swoosh! His magic patch on the seat of his pants took the hint and Jimmy found himself whizzing through space. With a bump he landed—on the deck of an old-time sailing ship! His eyes opened wide as he saw what was happening on board.

3—A band of ruffians had mutinied on the ship and over-powered the captain and his trusty men. The mutineers had run up the pirate flag and the leader was now ordering one of his men to lash the captain, helplessly tied to a dangling rope. It was then that the evil bosun noticed Jimmy. "Ho!" he roared. "Who's this come to interfere!" Unconsciously Jimmy raised his wooden sword as the bearded ruffian approached.

4—A bellow of laughter came from the bosun. "So it's sword-play you want?" he roared. "On guard then, dog!" Jimmy clumsily warded off an evil thrust with his wooden sword, but he knew how helpless he was. The cutlass flickered in and out far too quickly for Jimmy to see and suddenly his sword jerked in his hand. An evil grin flooded the bosun's weather-beaten face. He had cut Jimmy's wooden sword in two!

5—Jimmy groaned and dropped the useless handle. The bosun stepped towards him. Like lightning the lad turned and raced away down the deck. A wild yell of fury came from the bosun as he started in pursuit. "Wait till I catch you!" he roared. "I'll dangle you from the highest yard-arm!" Jimmy leaped for the shrouds at the side of the ship. The lad had never moved faster than he did then.

6—He was halfway up before the pirate had started to climb. But the evil bosun was no new hand at this game like Jimmy. He soon shortened the space between them. Scrambling up-wards, well beyond the crow's nest, Jimmy glanced down. Cut-lass between teeth, the bosun was barely a yard behind him. Jimmy's pulses were racing as he started to climb still further up the mast. Soon the bosun would be able to cut him down.

7—He kept climbing until at last he was stuck. Clinging to the mast with one hand, he desperately snatched his fountain pen from his pocket. The bosun gave an evil laugh as he raised his cutlass just as Jimmy jerked at the lever of the pen with his thumb. It had been newly filled and a thick stream of ink shot out—into the bosun's eye! The shock made him release his hold on the mast.

8—With a startled cry he dropped downwards. His cutlass fell with him. The men's faces on deck changed from grins to dismay as their leader dropped, howling, from the mast-top. They were too excited watching him to notice that the falling cutlass sheered through the rope holding the captain of the ship. In no time he managed to free himself now that his arms were loose enough to move his hands freely.

9—Stealthily he stepped behind one of the mutineers and swung an arm about the man's neck. The man's cry for help turned into a low gasp as the captain's arm tightened on his windpipe. The mutineer was helpless to prevent the captain helping himself to his cutlass and pistol. Jimmy was the only person aboard who noticed this quiet struggle as he slid quickly to the deck. The mutineers were watching their leader struggling in the water.

10—It was only when the captain shouted his order to lay down their arms that they awoke to the situation. By then it was too late. A steady hand covered them with a pistol which none of the yellow-livered mutineers dared to move against. Under the captain's orders Jimmy opened the deck house and freed his trusty men. A few of the mutineers threw a rope to the evil bosun and he was helped aboard.

11—Dripping wet, he faced the captain. He realised he was trapped, but a gleam of hope shone in his eyes as the captain spoke. "There's only one way to deal with traitors," he roared, and flung a rapier at the bosun's feet. "Here, take this" "A fight to the finish," the bosun thought. There was still a chance. He grabbed the rapier and thrust at the captain. The onlookers were silent as the steel clashed.

12—The swords were like flickering shafts of light. Once, twice, the captain drew blood, until the bosun could fight no longer. He threw down his sword and cried for mercy. With his disgruntled men he was tied up and locked away. "You made that possible," the captain said, turning to Jimmy. "Thanks for—" but that was as far as he got. Jimmy suddenly found himself back in modern times, thinking of his latest exciting adventure.

JIMMY AND HIS MAGIC PATCH

1—Jimmy Watson was in another fine pickle! His Magic Patch had landed him in a country where prehistoric monsters roamed. As he had been reading the "Adventure" at home he had wished he could have shared the thrilling adventures of Strang the Terrible. As he looked around him a huge brontosaurus reared its ugly head above the trees. It had seen Jimmy! With great speed for its size it started towards our horrified pal, and he rushed madly in the opposite direction towards a deep chasm.

2—As he heard the great brute pounding along beside him Jimmy raced towards a narrow archway of stone that spanned the cleft. Panting, red in the face, he reached it at last and madly rushed across. Every second it seemed that his feet would slip on the narrow bridge. Hundreds of feet below Jimmy glimpsed a raging torrent of foaming water—not a nice place to land into! Jimmy didn't stop running until he had gone quite a distance from the chasm.

3—Even then the roars made by the huge beast sent cold shivers down his spine. Luckily it couldn't cross the narrow bridge and slunk off. Jimmy pulled out his handkerchief and sat down on a large stone. Mopping his face, he looked at the "Adventure" again. "Gee!" he said. "This might be okay for a bloke like Strang, but it's too much for me." Suddenly Jimmy stopped thinking. The stone he was sitting on had moved.

4—His heart pounding madly like a sledgehammer, Jimmy felt himself lifted into the air. He had been sitting on a huge triceratops. It was a good job for Jimmy the brute didn't know he was there. As the huge beast, with two large horns sticking from its head, rose to its feet, Jimmy didn't know what to do. Thrusting his "Adventure" into his pocket, he thought about jumping off, but suddenly the huge animal started to run.

5—At that moment Jimmy noticed another monster racing full speed toward the animal he was kneeling on. Now the triceratops was going like an express train towards its opponent. It looked as if Jimmy might be squashed to pulp when the monsters met. Just as he was passing underneath a tree and the two monsters were but a few yards from each other he put his hand over his eyes and waited for the sickening impact.

6—A second before the beasts clashed together Jimmy felt himself being lifted into the tree. As he looked above him he saw he was held by the long hairy arm of a gorilla. "Out of the frying pan into the fire!" Jimmy thought as he saw its ugly face peer down at him. The two huge animals were now fighting some distance away and the gorilla hauled Jimmy up on to the branch on which it sat.

7—The unlucky lad shuddered as it showed its huge yellow teeth. He probably would have been better off where he had been a few minutes before, he thought. Just as he was wondering what was going to happen to him next the gorilla stood on the branch and, dangling Jimmy in space by his leg, beat on its massive chest with its other clenched fist. To Jimmy it seemed that the gorilla was challenging someone to fight.

8—That was just what happened! On the other side of a small stream Strang the Terrible stood. He had heard the challenge from the ape and now he noticed Jimmy dangling from the gorilla's hand. Clenching his fist, he beat on his broad chest, too, returning the challenge. Jimmy brightened up a little as he heard the world-famous strong man. It looked as if he still had a chance. Quickly Strang went into action.

9—He started to run towards Jimmy and the ape, taking huge strides which seemed to be yards long by Jimmy. Jumping the stream as if it were a mere trickle of water, Strange plunged into the thick undergrowth and in a remarkably short time reached the tree. Snarling with rage, the gorilla climbed from the tree, leaving Jimmy on one of the lower branches. He gave a startled cry as the gorilla swung out at Strang.

10—Jimmy needn't have worried. Strang didn't get his name for nothing. He cleverly dodged the swing and closed to grapple with the gorilla. Jimmy watched in horrified silence as the fight went on. Slowly but surely it seemed to Jimmy that Strang was gaining the upper hand, until at last no doubt was left in his mind. Jimmy saw Strang's muscles tense, then, swinging his arm back with lightning speed, he gave the gorilla an uppercut.

11—The thud of the blow could have been heard for a long distance. The gorilla's head snapped back with the tremendous punch. Its neck was broken, and the lifeless body measured its length on the rocky ground, where the huge bulk lay motionless. Strang was victorious! He helped Jimmy on to his shoulder, and waving his school cap in the air Jimmy cheered until he was hoarse. "Stop that awful row," said Strang with a grin.

12—"Tell me how you got here in the first place." Jimmy started to tell about the Magic Patch but he never got far. Suddenly he realised he was speaking to himself. He was back at home in modern times again, sitting back at the table with his "Adventure" in his hand just as he had been reading it before. "Oh, well," he said to himself, "I suppose I'll just have to be content reading about Strang again."

JIMMY'S MAGIC PATCH

Jimmy, out cycling one day, spied some men competing in an Archery Competition. "This looks fun," said Jimmy to himself, and stopped to watch the unusual contest. "If they were all dressed differently and wore feathers in their hats it would just be like the days of Robin Hood and his Merry Men. Sherwood Forest must have been an exciting place." Suddenly Jimmy said out loud:—"I wish I were living in those times, and could meet Robin Hood and Maid Marion, too."

Now on Jimmy's pants there was a big patch. But it wasn't just an ordinary patch. It was a MAGIC patch. And every time Jimmy wished a wish, the patch on his pants saw that the wish was granted. It never failed to oblige Jimmy, and sure enough it worked the trick once again, and suddenly Jimmy found himself on a small path cycling through a forest. There, right in front of him, he saw two monks beating up a man. Two horses grazed near by.

The Magic-Beano Book

The monks grabbed the bag that the poor man was clutching, then mounted and rode off on the horses. Jimmy approached the dazed man and asked if he could help. " These are robbers dressed as monks," the man said,"and they are the same ones who are waylaying and robbing all the poor people around here. If you would like to help, ride to Robin Hood in Sherwood Forest and tell him. I will follow. My name is Edwin."

Off Jimmy went on his bicycle, speeding through the trees till he came to a small clearing. There, sure enough, were Robin Hood and some of his Merry Men, and also Maid Marion. As Jimmy drew nearer he could see they were all enjoying an afternoon of sport, but at his approach, they looked up in great surprise and wonder. Robin Hood and company, of course, had never seen such a thing as a bicycle.

Jimmy's Magic Patch

At first, Robin and his followers were very wary, and then finding the excited Jimmy to be a friendly boy, they came closer. "I'll show you some trick-riding," said Jimmy, and was so thrilled at being able to show off in front of this famous man, that he quite forgot the message from Edwin. Laying a narrow track of leaves round a great oak tree, Jimmy began to cycle round faster and faster. The Merry Men were awe-struck. Then Edwin entered the clearing.

Jimmy jumped from his cycle and joined the others who had clustered round Edwin. The man was able to tell Robin Hood the direction the robbers had taken. "Would you not ride after them, Robin Hood? You are the only one who can teach them a lesson." Robin Hood looked worried. "Most of my horses are away with the rest of the Merry Men on a mission. The only two I kept for myself were stolen last night. I have no doubt those robbers took them."

"There's my bike, Robin Hood!" Jimmy cried. "I'll take you on the carrier." Robin Hood looked very doubtful at Jimmy's suggestion, but after a little persuasion finally consented. Robin was no lightweight, and it took Jimmy all his time to keep his balance. At last they were off to the cheers and laughter of the Merry Men. They sped along a woodland path. "We'll catch those rascals yet," said Jimmy, as they careered along.

Faster and faster Jimmy pedalled. On reaching the crest of a hill, Jimmy suddenly spied below the two robbers. "There they are!" he cried. "Get ready, Robin Hood!" "Look!" cried Robin, as he, too, saw them. "They are on my horses. I'll get the rascals for this, though we have to chase them for miles." Jimmy took a dim view of this remark, for already his legs were beginning to ache. But he pedalled bravely on.

Jimmy's Magic Patch

The strange chase brought them to a village. Seeing his chance, Robin Hood suddenly raised himself from the carrier as high as he dared. Fitting an arrow into his bow, he took aim. Jimmy tried to steer to even a course as possible, for he knew one false move on his part would be fatal to Robin Hood's plans. Whang! The arrow shot through the air, and suddenly one of the so-called monks found himself pinned by his cloak to a huge oak tree. The horse galloped on.

Robin and Jimmy did not waste any time on the rascal pinned to the tree, for the second man, realising his danger, had put a spurt on. But just as he was passing the stocks, Robin again took aim. Whang! Another arrow flew through the air, and the second robber was unseated and pinned by his cloak to one of the posts of the stocks. The villagers, by this time, were taking an interest in the proceedings, as many of them had been victims of the robbers' cruelty.

The Magic-Beano Book

Soon the rascals were firmly bound and led off. Robin Hood and Jimmy then picked up the robbers' sacks. The villagers gathered around, and Robin handed back the goods that had been stolen. By this time the horses, freed from the robbers, trotted back to Sherwood Forest by themselves. So Robin Hood and Jimmy had to return by bicycle— but this time Robin rode the bicycle and Jimmy was on the pillion!

And then the fun started! Robin Hood declared that this was an occasion for celebrating. And what a feast they had! There were huge roasts of beef, chickens, fruit of all kinds, and luscious tarts made by Maid Marion's fair hands. Never had Jimmy enjoyed such a picnic! He would be very loth to leave Robin Hood and his Merry Men, but he knew that sooner or later he must. At the moment, however, he was determined to enjoy himself, which he certainly did!

THE STORY OF
KIDNAPPED
BY ROBERT LOUIS STEVENSON

The Story of

TREASURE ISLAND

by Robert Louis Stevenson

THE STORY OF
ROBINSON CRUSOE
by
DANIEL DEFOE

CAST AWAY!

Survivors of the ship *Cabalva*, wrecked north of Mauritius in 1818, were stranded on a sandbank along with several live pigs. Until their rescue, the sailors, themselves short of food, fed the pigs on hairoil and scented soap salvaged from the cargo. The pigs thrived on the diet.

In 1929 a German doctor decided to go and live a castaway's life on a lonely island in the Pacific. He wasn't afraid of storms, or starvation or cannibals, but he was afraid of toothache—so he had all his teeth pulled out before he left Germany.

In 1846 the British steamer *Tweed* foundered on a reef in the Gulf of Mexico. A number of survivors reached the reef, which was perpetually washed by the sea. Using pieces of wreckage, they built a platform above the waves and lived there for five days until rescued by a Spanish ship.

At the end of last century, a Turk named Vassil settled on the uninhabited island of Oxia in the Sea of Marmora. Later, when the Turkish government used the island as a dumping ground for stray dogs, Vassil's life was often endangered by packs of the ravenous animals.

Because so many ships have been wrecked on Kangaroo Island, off the coast of South Australia, the Australian government maintains a permanent store of supplies there for the use of shipwrecked sailors. The stores include biscuits, condensed milk, salt, tea, matches and signal-rockets.

Wolves of the Spanish Main

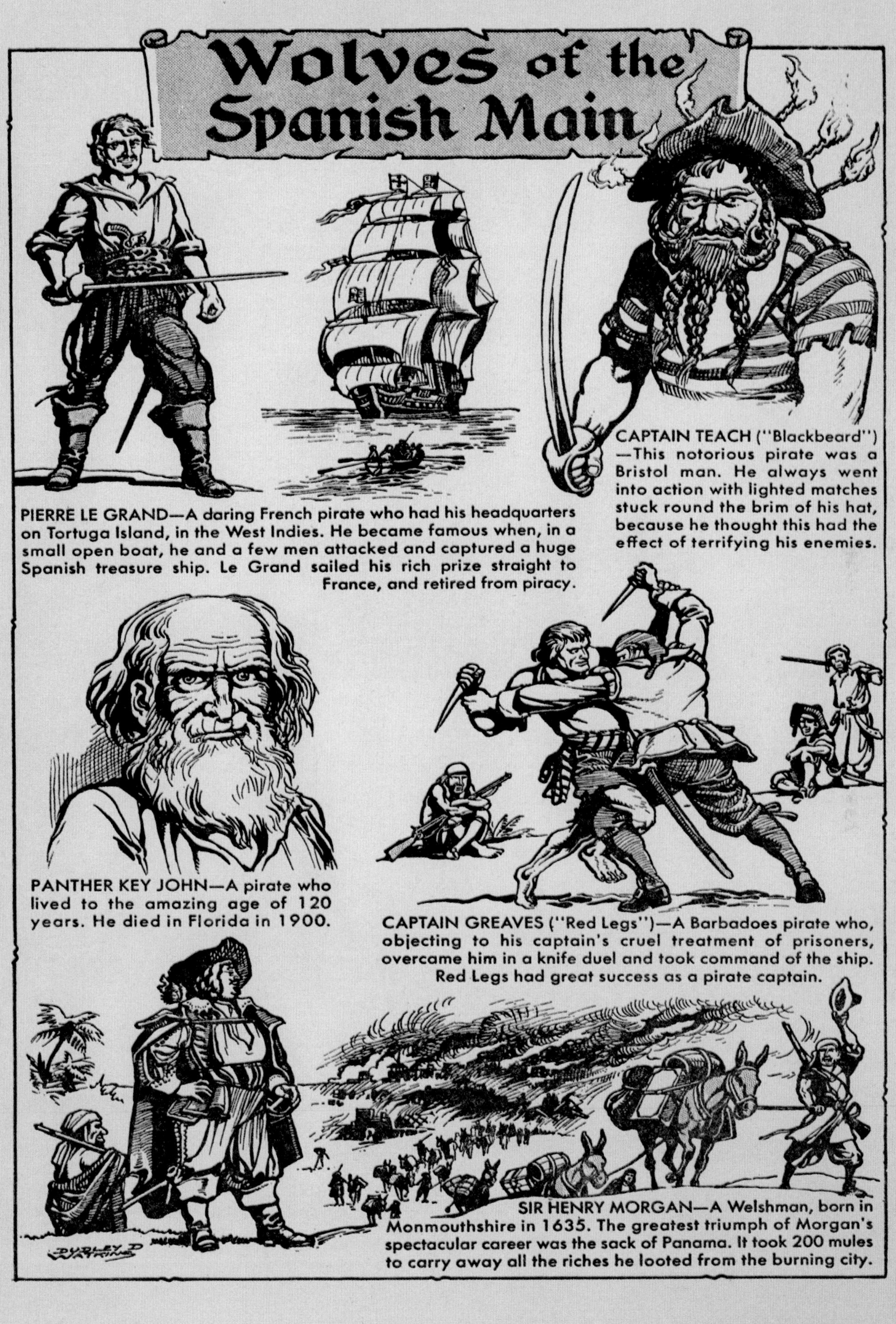

PIERRE LE GRAND—A daring French pirate who had his headquarters on Tortuga Island, in the West Indies. He became famous when, in a small open boat, he and a few men attacked and captured a huge Spanish treasure ship. Le Grand sailed his rich prize straight to France, and retired from piracy.

CAPTAIN TEACH ("Blackbeard")—This notorious pirate was a Bristol man. He always went into action with lighted matches stuck round the brim of his hat, because he thought this had the effect of terrifying his enemies.

PANTHER KEY JOHN—A pirate who lived to the amazing age of 120 years. He died in Florida in 1900.

CAPTAIN GREAVES ("Red Legs")—A Barbadoes pirate who, objecting to his captain's cruel treatment of prisoners, overcame him in a knife duel and took command of the ship. Red Legs had great success as a pirate captain.

SIR HENRY MORGAN—A Welshman, born in Monmouthshire in 1635. The greatest triumph of Morgan's spectacular career was the sack of Panama. It took 200 mules to carry away all the riches he looted from the burning city.

Soldiers' Uniforms & Arms
1742–1755
INFANTRY SOLDIER OF 1742 ARMED WITH FLINT-LOCK MUSKET AND INFANTRY SWORD.
DRUMMER IN INFANTRY REGIMENT, 1751.
TROOPER OF THE 8TH DRAGOONS, 1751.
FLINT-LOCK PISTOLS, USUALLY CARRIED BY OFFICERS AND MEN OF CAVALRY REGIMENTS.
FLINT-LOCK MUSKET.
CAVALRY SWORD.
GUARDS OFFICER, 1756.
BAYONET.
GRENADIER OF THE 9TH FOOT. GRENADIER COMPANIES WERE FORMED FROM THE BEST AND TALLEST MEN IN THE REGIMENT.

RED FERGIE'S "ARMY"

Red Fergie, the Jacobite, and young Col MacDonald, on their search for money and arms to aid the cause of Bonnie Prince Charlie, were making their way through a little wood. As they approached a clearing, they heard shouts, and quickly they both dropped to the ground. Crawling forward, they were able to see what was going on. And it wasn't a pleasant sight ! A few Highlanders who had been grazing their cattle some little distance from a small clachan, were being attacked and overpowered by a band of armed Red-Coats.

Quickly the Red-Coats proceeded to bind the Scotsmen with stout ropes. Then they marched through the village terrifying the women and children and collecting all the live-stock and provisions they could lay hands on. Red Fergie motioned to Col. " We'll follow," he whispered. " There must be something we can do." The Red-Coats, never thinking they were being followed, jeered at the Highlanders and joked among themselves. At last the Red-Coats stopped at the foot of a rocky incline and prepared to camp for the night.

Sentries were posted on several small hills round about, and the Red-Coats set about making a fire and preparing their evening meal. Red Fergie and young Col lay hidden behind a stone dyke. Suddenly, Red Fergie motioned young Col up the hillside. "Follow me," he whispered. "I've thought of a plan to rescue the Highlanders and make the Red-Coats look small. Listen, and I'll tell you what we'll do!"

Slowly and silently the two mounted the hillside. Young Col, who was carrying his bag-pipes under one arm, found the rocky hillside no obstacle, having been brought up among mountains. He turned once or twice to look down on the Red-Coats, and smiled to think of the shock in store for them. Red Fergie reached the top first and leant over to assist Col to safety. "We'll have to hurry," he remarked. "It will soon be dusk, and my plan won't work then."

Red Fergie's "Army"

"Collect all the small boulders and stones you can, and heap them up on the edge of the cliff," Red Fergie instructed. The two worked hard piling the boulders neatly on top of each other and making fair-sized cairns on the cliff-edge. It was a risky job, for, if one stone had rolled over, the Red-Coats would at once have been on the alert, and the complete surprise of the enemy was necessary for the success of the Jacobite's plan.

When the cairns had been completed, young Col turned to Red Fergie. "What do we do next?" he whispered excitedly. Red Fergie smiled. "Collect all the small fallen branches lying around, and sharpen one end of each to look like a bayonet." Red Fergie found a large branch and began to fix on to it the small branches which Col had sharpened. It didn't take the two long, and soon the spiked branches were fixed on the whole length of the log.

Red Fergie stepped towards one of the cairns. "Play a march on your pipes, Col," he whispered. "Make as much noise as possible," he added with a smile. Young Col picked up his pipes, and with great gusto played a rousing Highland march, while Red Fergie with a mighty heave pushed one of the stone cairns over the cliff edge. There was a crash and a great rumble of stones tore down the hillside. Quickly Red Fergie pushed over the second pile of stones.

Then young Col dropped his pipes and picked up one end of the prepared log, while Red Fergie took the other. "Slowly, now," whispered Red Fergie. "Make it look as though there was a whole army on the march." There was a slight dip in the cliff-edge, and, crouching, so that only the tops of the bayonet-like spikes were to be seen, they walked backwards and forwards. Red Fergie stopped at last. "That's fine, Col," he laughed. "You can lay it down now."

Red Fergie's "Army"

First, the stones rushing down the cliff-side put the Red-Coats on the alert. Then suddenly the noise of bag-pipes drifted down to them. "The Highlanders are coming!" one of the Red-Coats yelled; and there, sure enough, to their amazed eyes appeared what looked like the bayonets of an army slowly marching past. The Highland captives grinned. They couldn't understand how relief had come so quickly, but there was no doubt the Red-Coats were scared.

The Red-Coat officer was shouting his commands. "We are outnumbered. We must flee." He had no need to give the order, for already his men were on the run. Some picked up their guns and swords, but others were too intent on escape and left them lying. The soldiers' only concern was escape. The Highland prisoners were gleeful. The tables had certainly turned, and they laughed at the undignified retreat of the Red-Coats.

The Magic-Beano Book

The Highlanders waited eagerly for the troops to descend the cliff-edge, and their amazement, when only a man and a boy appeared, was amusing to see. "Where is the army?" they asked. "Here," Red Fergie laughed, and he told them of the trick young Col and he had worked. "But we must hurry," added Red Fergie. "These Red-Coats will have gone for help and we must not be here when they return." Quickly the Highlanders were untied.

Red Fergie, Col and the Highlanders then collected all the live-stock and goods the Red-Coats had taken from the clachan. Slowly they made their way homewards, but before they entered it, two of the Highlanders hoisted Red Fergie up and carried him shoulder high into the village. In this triumphant fashion they entered the clachan where a welcome, as rousing as Col's bagpipe music, was given them by the overjoyed and grateful villagers.

GULLIVER

THE PARAFFIN OIL PLOT

ONE day when Gulliver was sitting on the beach dreaming of home, and wondering if he would ever see his own country again, a tiny little man came running down the beach yelling:

"Gulliver, something's been washed up on the beach away along the coast there. A messenger has just arrived at the Royal Palace to tell the king. He says it's a giant cask that has been washed up, and the king thinks it must have come from your ship which was sunk."

"That is quite likely, Snippy," said Gulliver, picking up the little man and rising to his feet. "We'd better go and ask the messenger to guide us to where this cask is lying!"

The messenger did so and Gulliver found that it was a cask containing paraffin oil.

"Yes, it's from my ship, all right," he said as he examined it.

"But what is it?" demanded Snippy, for paraffin oil was quite unknown in Lilliput.

"It's stuff which burns very brightly in lamps," said Gulliver. "I will give it to the king as a present!"

With the cask on one shoulder and with little Snippy sitting on the other, Gulliver strode off in the direction of the Royal Palace.

When he reached the town he had to step very carefully over the streets of houses.

On reaching the Royal Palace, however, both Gulliver and Snippy were startled by the frightful commotion which was going on.

Servants and courtiers were running hither and thither about the courtyard, and King Tiny himself was standing on the highest balcony of the Royal Palace, wringing his hands and crying :

" Oh, what will I do—oh, what will I do? My poor Griselda. Oh, what will I do?"

" Why, Your Majesty, whatever has happened?" cried Gulliver in alarm, stooping down over the Royal Palace.

" My daughter Griselda has been kidnapped and carried off by that wicked scoundrel, Baron Bawler !" cried the king, wringing his tiny hands. " She was out riding this afternoon when he and his wicked band fell upon her and her servants and carried her off !"

More than once Gulliver had severely punished this Baron and his men for their misdeeds, and the whole robber band simply hated him.

The Baron's Threat.

" DON'T you worry about him carrying off your daughter, Your Majesty," cried Gulliver. " I will go to his stronghold at once and rescue her for you. What is more, I will bring that horrid little Baron and his men back here so that you can mete out to them the punishment they deserve."

" No, no, no !" cried the king in despair. " That is just what you must not do. The Baron has sworn that if you go near his castle I will never see my dear Griselda again !"

"What?" roared Gulliver in a terrible voice.

" Yes," cried the king, wringing his tiny hands. " That is one of the reasons why he has carried her off. He says that not only must I pay him a ransom of one thousand pieces of gold for her return, but that you must leave Lilliput never to return. He says if you approach within a mile of his castle Griselda will be doomed !"

" I'll go and pull his castle to pieces about his wicked little head !" roared Gulliver. " I've never heard such cheek. I'll teach him to order me to leave Lilliput !"

" No, no, you mustn't touch him," cried the king in terror. " If you start pulling his castle to pieces—if you even go near it—it will mean that I will never see my daughter again. The wicked villain means what he says. I know he does. You cannot hurt the Baron without dooming my daughter to some dreadful fate."

Gulliver was silent for a few moments. Then he straightened up.

" I see," he said. " Well, I must think this out, Your Majesty. I'm not going to let a wicked little creature like Baron Bawler get the better of me. And don't you pay that ransom of one thousand pieces of gold."

" I must, I must !" wailed King Tiny. " A messenger is riding with the ransom even now !"

" Oh, is he?" said Gulliver grimly. " Well, I must be off, Your Majesty !"

The Frightened Messenger.

WITH that Gulliver turned away. Stepping very carefully over the streets of little houses he strode off into the country with the cask of paraffin oil on one shoulder and little Snippy on the other.

" Where are we off to, Gulliver?" cried Snippy as Gulliver covered hill and dale in his stride.

" We're going to get hold of that messenger with the thousand pieces of gold first," said Gulliver. " I'm not going to let the king be robbed by that horrid little Bawler. Ah, there's the messenger over there !"

He pointed to a little Lilliputian who, wearing the king's livery and mounted on a little horse, was riding swiftly in the direction of Baron Bawler's stronghold.

With four more long strides Gulliver caught up with the little rider. Bending down he plucked him neatly from the saddle with his finger and thumb.

" Stop—let me down !" cried the rider, kicking and struggling in Gulliver's fingers. " I'm riding on the king's business !"

" I know you are !" chuckled Gulliver. " But that's all right. I'm on the king's business as well. I'm not only going to save him a thousand pieces of gold, but I'm going to rescue the fair Griselda for him and also capture horrid little Baron Bawler. Now you give me the bag of gold and trot off back to the Royal Palace !"

"But I daren't !" cried the little rider.

"The king will be ever so angry with me !"

"Tell the king that I sent you back and that I'll be back in the morning myself with Griselda and Baron Bawler and his band,"

"Help!" howled the terrified Baron and his men. "Put the magic flames out!"

said Gulliver. " Now give me the gold and off you go !"

The rider didn't want to give Gulliver the gold although he knew that Gulliver and the king were the closest of friends. But Gulliver took the little bag of gold from him with the greatest of ease and set him down in the saddle of his horse again.

Waiting until the rider was galloping back the way he had come, Gulliver placed the cask of paraffin oil on its end on the ground and sat down on it.

Then taking Snippy from his shoulder he placed him on his knee and said :

" If only I could go near that castle, Snippy, I could pull it to pieces and rescue the Princess Griselda. But I cannot do that because if I do, and if Baron Bawler sees me, the Princess will be doomed. So we've got to use guile !"

" What's guile?" demanded Snippy.

" Cunning and craftiness," chuckled Gulliver. " Now you listen to me, Snippy. This is my plan and you'll have to help me !"

The Moat of Paraffin.

SNIPPY listened very carefully to what Gulliver had to say. But when Gulliver had finished Snippy burst out :

" But that means that you will go to the castle after all, Gulliver !"

" Only after darkness has fallen," chuckled Gulliver. " Then I will creep up so quietly that neither Baron Bawler nor his men will know I am anywhere around. I'm certainly not going to lay a finger on the castle, because that would mean the end of poor Princess Griselda. I'll do everything so quietly that no one will ever know I've been anywhere near the castle."

Waiting until the last light in the Baron's stronghold had gone out that night, Gulliver crept quietly towards the castle on his hands and knees.

He had Snippy perched on his head and he was rolling the cask of paraffin silently along in front of him.

When he reached the moat which surrounded the Baron's stronghold, Gulliver paused and listened intently. But not a sound broke the stillness.

With a soft chuckle Gulliver took his knife from his pocket and started to dig a channel in the side of the moat. This channel led to some sloping ground, and very soon the water from the moat was running away down the slope to be soaked up in the soft ground below.

Waiting till the moat was quite empty, Gulliver silently filled in the channel which he had dug. Then he took the stopper out of the cask of paraffin, and poured the paraffin into the moat until it was at the same level as the water had been.

" That's done it, Snippy !" he chuckled. " Now I've got to leave the rest to you !"

" Don't you worry," said Snippy. " I know what to do !"

Without the slightest idea of what had been going on outside the castle during the night, Baron Bawler woke up the next morning and tugged the little bell-rope by the side of his bed.

" Has King Tiny sent that ransom of a thousand pieces of gold yet?" he bawled at the servant who answered the ring.

" No, sire," said the servant timidly.

" Then he'd better hurry up !" roared the Baron, bounding from bed in a very great rage and rushing to the window to see if there was any sign of a rider.

There wasn't. But as the Baron popped his furious face out of the window he saw little Snippy standing on the other side of the moat.

Black Magic.

" HI, you !" yelled Snippy. " I've got a message for you from Gulliver !"

" Him?" sneered the Baron. " What's he got to say, the big, stupid man-mountain, that he is !"

" He says unless you release Princess Griselda at once he'll put a magic spell on you !" yelled Snippy.

" Oh, will he?" snarled the Baron. " He doesn't know any more magic than I do."

" That's what you think !" yelled Snippy. " You'll soon change your mind when you see the magic arrow which he has given me. This magic arrow will set the water in your moat on fire."

" Ha, ha, ha ! Just hark at that !" roared the Baron with a scornful laugh. " A magic arrow that will set water on fire, indeed ! Don't talk such rubbish !"

" Will you release the Princess Griselda?" cried Snippy.

" No, I won't !" roared the Baron.

" Then here goes !" cried Snippy.

With these words he snatched up an arrow. This arrow had a wisp of cloth tied to it that had been soaked in paraffin. Setting fire to the cloth Snippy hastily fitted the arrow into his bow and fired it into the moat.

Now, as you know, the moat was full of paraffin instead of water. The Baron never guessed that, of course, because he didn't know what paraffin was.

All he did know was that the instant the arrow fell into the moat, the " water " in the moat burst into flames which spread so swiftly that within a few moments the castle was surrounded by a leaping wall of flame.

The flame shot straight up, of course, and didn't hurt the castle except to make it uncomfortably hot for the terrified Baron and his men.

" Help !" they howled. " Stop ! Put the magic flames out and we'll release the Princess !"

The flames died down and went out as the paraffin in the moat burned away. Then Gulliver appeared, striding swiftly to the scene.

" You've seen my magic arrow burn water !" he roared. " Now I'm going to show you how it can burn stone. It's going to burn your castle down !"

" No, no, mercy, help !" roared the Baron and his men, rushing madly out of the castle into the courtyard.

" Then have the Princess Griselda released at once, you horrid little creature !" roared Gulliver, bending swiftly down and snatching up the Baron between his finger and thumb.

The terrified Baron ordered his men to bring the Princess out of her dungeon. They did so, and Gulliver picked her up and placed her gently in the pouch at his waist.

Then he grabbed a couple of handfuls of the Baron's men and strode off to the Royal Palace with them, the Baron and the Princess.

Needless to say the king was overjoyed to see his daughter safe and sound again. As for the Baron and his men they were cast into one of the dungeons of the Royal Palace, and left there to think over their misdeeds.

Picture excerpt taken from 'The Victory of the Little Ships', The Skipper Book for Boys, 1948.

LORD SNOOTY AND HIS PALS

LORD SNOOTY AND HIS PALS
LORD MARMADUKE — "SNOOTY" TO YOU!
ROSIE.
HAIRPIN HUGGINS.
SKINNY LIZZIE.
SCRAPPER SMITH.
"HAPPY" HUTTON.
GERTIE THE GOAT

YES, SNOOTY, THAT'S OUR FAMILY TREE AND YOU SEE YOUR GREAT GRANDMOTHER'S UNCLE'S COUSIN WAS A SCOTSMAN!
THE BUNKERTON FAMILY TREE
THEN I'VE GOT SCOTS BLOOD! I CAN WEAR TARTAN! I KNOW WHAT I'LL DO! I'LL GET A PIPE BAND FOR HOSPITAL WEEK.
NEXT DAY
THIS IS GREAT! WEARING SCOTS CLOTHES AND PLAYING BAGPIPES!
YES, WELL PRACTISE LIKE THIS ALL DAY FOR THE HOSPITAL WEEK PROCESSION TO-MORROW!
I'M PLAYING "ANNIE LAURIE"
OH? I DIDN'T KNOW I THOUGHT IT WAS "COCK ROBIN"
HUH! THEY AR-R-NA SCOTS! THEY'VE NAE RICHT TAE WEAR-R THE TAR-R-TAN!
WE MAUN PIT THEM TAE THE TEST!
SQUEAK
SKATES
THESE SKATES HAVE COME IN HANDY!

LATER.
CAN ONY O' YE ANSWER THESE QUESTIONS?
WHA'S RABBIE BURNS? WHIT IS HAGGIS? WIS ROB ROY A MACGREGOR OR A MACTAVISH? WHIT IS PARRITCH? DAE YE PIT SALT ON IT? CAM YE FRAE ECCLEFECHAN OR INVERARITY? CAN YE SAY "IT'S A BRAW BRICHT MUNELICHT NICHT THE NICHT?"
IF YE CANNA, WE'LL KEN YE'RE NO SCOTSMEN!
I DON'T KNOW WHAT HAGGIS IS!
NOR PARRITCH!
WHO'S ROB ROY?

SO YE CANNA ANSWER WIR QUESTIONS — WELL, WE'LL TELL YE! RABBIE BURNS WIS A SCOTS POET. HAGGIS IS A PUDDING PARRITCH IS PORRIDGE, IF YE'RE A SCOTSMAN YE PIT SALT ON IT AN' NOT SUGAR! AN' ROB ROY WIS A MᶜGREGOR!
OH!
IS ZAT SO!
BLIMEY!
GREAT SCOT!

THE SCOTSMEN HAVEN'T ASKED US ANY QUESTIONS YET AND WE COULDN'T ANSWER THEM IF THEY DID! BUT LISTEN — I'VE GOT AN IDEA!
WE'RE SORRY, LADY MATILDA, BUT LORD SNOOTY AND HIS FREENDS ARE NO TAE WEAR-R THE TAR-R-TAN — THEY'RE NO' SCOTS — BUT WHIT ABOOT THE ITHER TWA WEE LADDIES? WE'VE NO' TESTED THEM YET!
THEY'LL BE ALONG SHORTLY, I EXPECT!

WHA DARE MEDDLE WI' US? WE'RE SCOTS! LISTEN TAE WIR SANG!
THE MAC SNITCH AND MAC SNATCH WULL SING A DUET!

BONNIE ANNIE LAURIE
AYE, MAN! THAE TWA ARE SCOTS! THEY CAN WEAR-R THE TAR-RTAN!
SOB
?

CLAP CLAP
WALKING BACKWARDS
BOW

HA! HA! HA! THAT GRAMOPHONE RECORD OF THE TWO MᶜPHERSONS YOU PLAYED UNDER YOUR TARTAN FAIRLY KIDDED THOSE SCOTSMEN!

THE HOSPITAL WEEK PARADE
LOOK! SNITCHY AND SNATCHY ARE COLLECTING ALL THE MONEY! WE'RE GETTING NOTHING!
STUCH
SQUEAK
CONK
QUICK, SNITCH! PUT ON ANOTHER RECORD OF BAGPIPES!
A GRAND PIPER! A TRUE SON O' THE HIGHLANDS! I WID GIE THEM A SAXPENCE — IF YE COULD LEN' ME ANE!

LORD SNOOTY
AND
HIS PALS
LORD MARMADUKE— "SNOOTY" TO YOU!
ROSIE.
HAIRPIN HUGGINS.
SKINNY LIZZIE.
SCRAPPER SMITH.
"HAPPY" HUTTON.
GERTIE THE GOAT

EVERY MAN, WOMAN AND CHILD IN STALINGRAD FOUGHT TO SAVE THE CITY! THAT'S WHY THE KING PRESENTED STALINGRAD WITH A SWORD OF HONOUR!
LET'S GET SOME TOGGLE ROPES AND DO SOME TOWN FIGHTING! WE CAN USE THE BOMBED AREA IN THE TOWN!
WE'LL SHOW 'EM!

LATER! GEE! SNOOTY AND HIS GANG ARE PLAYING AT TOWN FIGHTING!
GOSH! THESE KIDS ARE BETTER THAN MY HOME GUARD MEN!

LORD SNOOTY, I'M GOING TO GET MY MEN ON PARADE AND I WANT YOU TO GIVE THEM A DEMONSTRATION OF STREET FIGHTING!
O.K. CAPTAIN WE'LL BE WAITING FOR YOU!
WE'RE GIVING THAT DEMONSTRATION GET YOUR CATAPULTS READY!

LET THEM HAVE IT, BOYS— FIRE!
WANG
PING
CLONK
RETREAT! THE ENEMY ARE DUG IN AND HAVE GREATER FIRE POWER!
REARGUARD ACTION

THE KELLIES ARE GUARDING THE RUINS, BUT YOU KIDS WILL GET PAST THE GUARDS, THEN— DO YOUR STUFF!
GRIM

HEY! MY MA LIVES UP HERE— YOU CAN'T KEEP US OUT?
O.K. PASS THROUGH!

QUICK! SHOVE THE NAIL STUDDED PLANKS UNDER THE TOP MATTRESS!

WE WERE INVADED AND DRIVEN OUT CAPTAIN BUT WE'VE MADE PLANS TO RECAPTURE THE PLACE. WE WANT YOU TO ASK FOR A JUMPING DEMONSTRATION FIRST
VERY WELL

PLEASE GIVE THE JUMPING DEMONSTRATION FIRST!
YOU GET SIR!

OOH!

WOW! HELP! MY PANTS ARE PERFORATED!
BANDAGES QUICK! WHERE'S THE FIRST AID POST?
OOH!
AFTER THEM, BOYS! TAKE THEM PRISONER DON'T LET THEM GET ACROSS THE DNIEPER!
WE WILL SOON GIVE OUR DEMONSTRATION NOW SIR!

PRISONER OF WAR CAMP
HOORAY! JOLLY GOOD!
I NOW HAVE PLEASURE IN PRESENTING YOU WITH A SWORD OF HONOUR!

BRING OUT THE NEXT PRISONER!
HOWL
SLAP

LORD SNOOTY AND HIS PALS
LORD MARMADUKE- "SNOOTY" TO YOU!
ROSIE.
HAIRPIN HUGGINS.
SKINNY LIZZIE.
SCRAPPER SMITH.
"HAPPY" HUTTON.
GERTIE THE GOAT.

AH! THERE'S MR WATKINS, THE MAN WHO DRAWS US FOR "THE BEANO" - LET'S ASK HIM TO TEACH US TO DRAW.
HI-YA MR WATKINS!
HULLO, BOYS!

SAY, MR WATKINS! WILL YOU TEACH US HOW TO DRAW?
I'M SORRY, KIDS, BUT I'M TOO BUSY JUST NOW - TELL YOU WHAT I'LL DO THOUGH - I'LL GIVE YOU THIS BOOK ON DRAWING TO STUDY!

LISTEN TO THIS - WHEN DRAWING FOR COMIC PAPERS ALWAYS DRAW PEOPLE FUNNIER THAN THEY REALLY ARE, E.G.- IF DRAWING A THIN BOY MAKE HIM VERY THIN ETC.
HOW TO DRAW

GEE! WATTY'S BEEN MAKING US LOOK WORSE THAN WE REALLY ARE!
COME ON, GANG! LET'S GO AND TELL THIS TWISTER WATKINS TO DRAW US NICELY, OR ELSE WE'LL BEAT HIM UP!
HUH! THE IDEA! MAKE A FOOL OF ME, WOULD HE?
WATTY'S HOUSE

WE'VE FOUND OUT FROM THIS BOOK WHY WE LOOK SUCH SILLY IDIOTS IN THE "BEANO" EVERY WEEK - IF YOU'D ONLY DRAW US PROPERLY FOLKS WOULDN'T LAUGH AT US EVERY WEEK!
YES, YOU'LL DRAW ME HANDSOME NEXT TIME OR ELSE -

WHY, YOU CHEEKY YOUNG SCOUNDRELS! I'LL SHOW YOU WHO'S BOSS HERE! JUST FOR THAT I'LL DRAW THE GASWORKS GANG INSTEAD OF YOU FOR "THE BEANO"!
HO! STOP SHOVING!
OUCH! IT WOULD BE A HOLLY BUSH!

LATER!
SMILE PLEASE (IF YOU CAN) WHILE I DRAW A CARTOON OF YOU, YOU'RE THE HEROES OF IT, YOU KNOW!
LOOK! THERE'S THOSE GASWORKS ROTTERS POSING FOR MR WATKINS! I'LL FOOL 'EM YET!

BACK AT THE CASTLE
I'LL DRAW A CARTOON TOO - BUT IT WON'T BE THE KIND THOSE TOUGHS WILL LIKE!
HA! HA! THAT'S AWFULLY FUNNY, SNOOTY.

COME THROUGH TO THE LOUNGE FOR A CUP OF TEA, BOYS, I'LL FINISH THE CARTOON AFTERWARDS!
NOW'S MY CHANCE TO TAKE WATTY'S CARTOON AWAY AND LEAVE MINE INSTEAD!
GEE, THANKS!

BACK IN THE STUDIO
DO YOU MIND IF WE HAVE A LOOK AT THE CARTOON MR WATKINS?
NOT AT ALL!
NOW FOR THE FUN!

HEY YOU! TAKE OUR PHOTOS AND MAKE IT SNAPPY!
BAH! YOUR UGLY MUGS HAVE CRACKED MY CAMERA
CRACK!
SPLIT AND SNATCH
MOUSE
HOWL! WE'RE FRIGHTENED TO DEATH OF MICE - HOWL! SCREAM!
HA! HA! JUST LIKE A COUPLE OF GIRLS!
WE'LL SHOW YOU WE'RE NOT CISSIES!
5 MINUTES LATER
Z-ZZ
HUH! YOU CAN'T EVEN FIGHT!

MAKE A FOOL OF US WOULD YOU? TAKE THAT!
BUT-BUT!
HO! HO! THE TOUGHS DON'T SEEM TO LIKE YOUR DRAWING MR WATKINS!
-AND THAT.

GOSH! WHAT NASTY BRUTES THOSE TOUGHS WERE! I'VE LEARNT MY LESSON, BOYS - I'LL NEVER DRAW ANYONE ELSE BUT YOU!
HO! HO! WE'RE SURE GLAD TO HEAR THAT MR WATKINS!
LOOK! THE NAUGHTY BOY'S BEEN FIGHTING!
HA! HA! I COULDN'T HAVE LICKED HIM BETTER MYSELF!
BU-ZZZ

Desperate Dan

DESPERATE DAN

DESPERATE DAN

THE SCHOOL JANITOR IS OFF ILL, DAN! COULD YOU DO HIS JOB TOMORROW?
WHY, SURE!
SCHOOL

NEXT MORNING
I'LL GET THE SCHOOL FIRE GOING! HUH! WHAT A PESKY LITTLE BOILER!

THIS WATER TANK WILL MAKE A FAR BETTER BOILER!

I'LL BREAK UP A FEW SCHOOL DESKS TO MAKE A REAL BIG FIRE!

NOW I'LL SCRUB THE CLASSROOM FLOOR! HUH! THIS INK STAIN IS TAKING A BIT OF SCRUBBING OUT!

WOW! I'VE SCRUBBED A HOLE IN THE FLOOR! THAT INK STAIN MUST HAVE BEEN A KNOT IN THE WOOD!

ORDER IN CLASS— HERE'S TEACHER!
WOW! THERE'S A HOLE IN THE FLOOR!

SORRY, SIR!
WE'LL BE MORE CAREFUL OR YOU'LL GET THE SACK!
HAW! HAW!

TRY AND CLEAN THE SKY-LIGHT WITHOUT BREAKING IT!
WHAT'S THAT? I CAN'T HEAR!

BEG PARDON? OH, SORRY, SIR!
CRASH
WOW

LATER! DAN! IT'S TOO HOT IN HERE! GO AND FIX THAT BOILER!
O.K., SIR!
HOT

WOW! IT'S BOILING LIKE FURY!
S-S-SS

BANG

JEEPERS CREEPERS! THE BOILER'S BURST AND WRECKED THE SCHOOL!
SWOOSH
SCHOOL

DAN! YOU'RE FIRED! BOYS, TAKE FOUR WEEKS' HOLIDAY WHILE THE SCHOOL'S BEING REPAIRED!
WHOOPEE! GOOD OLD DAN! YOU'VE GOT US A HOLIDAY! WHOOPEE!

DESPERATE DAN

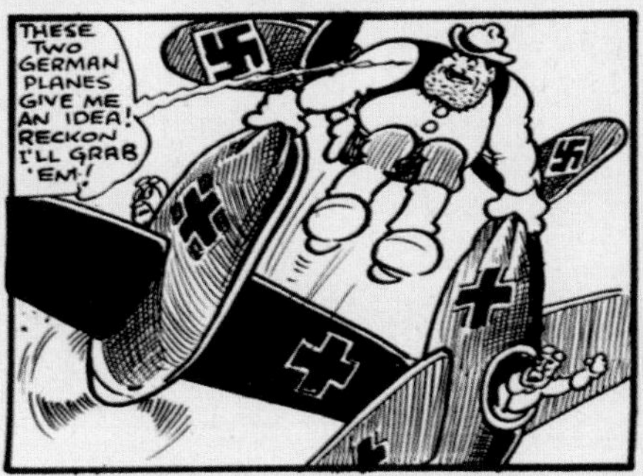

BIFFO
THE BEAR

Watkins' first cover star, Biffo the Bear, burst on to the Beano scene on 24th January, 1948. Following Beano Editor, RD Low's favour for monochromatic cover characters (so as to stand out against the colourful world they inhabit) Biffo was born in black and white, the only colour being his trademark red dungarees.

Replacing Big Eggo on the covers, Biffo maintained the former's anthropomorphisms and lack of speech balloons, with strips often centring around the wily bear's occupational misadventures.

Starting with issue No.575, Biffo shared his covers with his human friend, Buster, who was often his co-conspirator in adventures, and would eventually get a one-off strip, Biffo and Buster.

HIP HURRAH! HIP HOORAY!
BIFFO BEAR is here to-day!

THE BEANO COMIC
2D
Nº 327. JAN. 24th 1948

Biffo the Bear

GRAND CONCERT STARTS AT 2 P.M.

CONCERT HALL

SECOND-HAND MUSICAL INSTRUMENTS BOUGHT AND SOLD
FOR SALE

MUSIC 321

GRAND CONCERT STARTS AT 2 P.M.

EXIT

EXIT

CONCERT HALL

THE BEANO COMIC

APRIL
1

THE BEANO COMIC
2ᴰ
No. 332. APRIL 3ᴿᴰ 1948

Biffo
the
Bear
RED AND WHITE STRIPED PAINT
BIFFO'S HAIR CUTTING SALOON

APRIL FOOL

BROWN
BARBER WANTED

BARBER WANTED

BARBER WANTED

RASP
FOR BIFFO

THE BEANO COMIC

2ᴰ

No 336. MAY 29th 1948

GULLIVER

BARON BAWLER'S BLACK-OUT

GULLIVER was a sailor whose ship had been sunk in a great storm and he had been cast away on Lilliput, the land of little people. Gulliver was an ordinary sized man but he seemed like a giant to the little people, and they called him the man-mountain.

One day when he was taking a stroll in the country, he saw one of the tiny Lilliputians riding furiously towards him on a little horse.

"Oh, Gulliver!" yelled the little rider, reining in his horse at Gulliver's feet. "I've got some news for you!"

"Have you, indeed?" said Gulliver in surprise, wondering what news he could be bringing.

He bent down and lifted the little fellow gently from his horse between his finger and thumb.

"Now what's this news?" he asked, standing the Lilliputian on the palm of his hand.

"There's a monster box coming ashore away over by the beach," cried the Lilliputian, pointing with his tiny hand. "It's such an enormous box that it can only have come from your giant ship. It's nearly as big as the king's Royal Palace."

"Is the box empty or is there anything in it?" asked Gulliver.

"We can't tell," cried the Lilliputian. "The sides are much too high for us to see into the box. All our fishing boats are keeping well clear of it in case it bumps into them and sinks them."

"Very well, I'll go and get it," said Gulliver. "Thank you very much for telling me about it."

He put the Lilliputian back on his horse, then strode off towards the box which was bobbing up and down in the sea.

The Empty Box.

WHEN he reached the beach, Gulliver saw a great crowd of little Lilliputian fishermen standing there staring in awe at the box which was, to them, as big as a fortress.

Taking off his shoes and stockings, Gulliver waded out into the sea and seized the big, wooden box. To his disappointment it was quite empty. Gulliver had been hoping that it would contain something which might be of use to him in this land where everything was so very tiny.

"Never mind, I'll be able to make some use of it," he said to himself as he placed the box on his shoulder and waded back to the beach. "It'll do for firewood, if for nothing else."

It had come from his sunken ship, all right. He knew that, and, as he set it down on the beach and pulled on his shoes and stockings, the Lilliputian fishermen gathered round it, crying :

"What are you going to do with it, Gulliver?"

"It'll make a grand big house for somebody, Gulliver !"

"It's big enough for a Town Hall. We could have meetings and dances in it, Gulliver."

"Yes, I expect you could," chuckled Gulliver. "I'll give it to the King and see what he suggests doing with it."

Having put his shoes and stockings on, Gulliver rose to his feet. Then putting the box on his shoulder again, he strode off in the direction of the Royal Palace, covering hill and dale in his stride.

Suddenly he halted, staring down at a tiny little wayside cottage which was burning fiercely.

It was the work of a moment for Gulliver to put down the box and whip off his jacket which he flung over the burning cottage, smothering the flames.

By pressing his jacket down on the flames, he soon put them out. Then to make certain that the little smouldering beams and rafters would not catch fire again, he strode off to a nearby lake and returned with a shoe full of water which he poured over the cottage.

"Oh, thank you, Gulliver, thank you," sobbed a tiny little voice, and Gulliver saw a peasant woman sitting crying near the cottage. "How good you are to save my cottage from being burned to the ground."

Gulliver is Angry.

BENDING down, Gulliver picked the little old woman gently up between his finger and thumb.

"How did your cottage catch fire?" he asked.

"It was that wicked Baron Bawler and his men," sobbed the woman. "They came riding along this way and because I had no silver or money to give them, they set fire to my cottage and rode away laughing like anything."

"Oh, they did, did they?" said Gulliver with a frown. "I'm sick and tired of the way that wicked little Baron treats you poor country folks. I've punished him before for his misdeeds, but this time I will teach the little rascal a lesson which he will not forget in a hurry !"

Baron Bawler, as Gulliver well knew, was just about the nastiest, meanest and cruellest little man in the whole of Lilliput.

He and his robber band were the terror of the countryside. They were always harrowing the poor and defenceless and more than once Gulliver had severely punished them for their misdeeds.

"Which way did the rascals go?" he asked the little peasant woman.

"That way," said the woman, pointing away along the road in the direction of the Baron's castle. "They seemed to be on their way back to their stronghold."

"Very well," said Gulliver, placing her gently down on the ground again. "I'll attend to them. Don't you worry about your cottage. I'll see that it is rebuilt for you and that wicked Baron Bawler pays you in gold for the damage he has done."

With that, Gulliver shouldered his big, empty box again and strode off in the direction of the Baron's stronghold.

As he strode along, thinking how best he could punish the Baron and his robber band

At length a hole was cut in the side of the box and Baron Bawler popped his head out.

for this latest wickedness of theirs, he gave a sudden start, then burst out laughing.

" I've got it !" he gleefully told himself. " Ha, ha, ha ! I know what I'll do !"

Then setting down the box, he sat down and waited patiently until darkness should fall.

When it was quite dark, Gulliver picked up his box and started on his way again. Very soon he saw in front of him the lighted windows of Baron Bawler's castle.

The Baron thought his castle was no end of a fine stronghold. So it was to the Lilliputians, but when Gulliver stood beside it the highest turrets scarcely reached his knees.

Reaching the castle, Gulliver stooped down in the darkness and stood a few moments, listening intently. To his ears came the sound of revelry from inside the castle, and Gulliver knew that the Baron and his robber band were feasting and probably laughing about the poor woman's cottage which they had burned that morning.

Is It 12 Midnight?

WITH a chuckle Gulliver straightened up. Then turning his big, empty box upside down he placed it over the castle.

The box was so big that it went right over the castle and if you had come along and seen the box standing there, you would never have dreamt that there was a castle underneath.

" I'll have to wait until morning before anything happens," chuckled Gulliver, seating himself on the upturned box. " But I don't mind that."

Seeing that it was pitch dark outside, the Baron and his men never dreamt for a moment that a huge box had been placed over their castle and they went to bed that night without the slightest idea as to what had happened.

The Baron slept very soundly until morning, lying snoring his horrid little head off. He woke up at length, and, to his surprise, everything was still dark.

" That's queer," thought the Baron. " It must be earlier than I thought."

He turned over and went off to sleep again. When next he woke up everything was still pitch black outside.

" Whatever is the matter?" thought the Baron crossly. " It must be morning by this time !"

Getting out of bed, he lit his little bedroom lamp and poked his head out of the window. But everything was as black as pitch.

The Baron then looked at his watch. As he did so he gave a violent start. For the hour was twelve o'clock, but whether it was twelve o'clock at night or twelve o'clock in the morning the Baron couldn't for the life of him say.

" It must still be night," he muttered. " It can't be anything else. But I could have sworn that I've been asleep for hours and hours."

Seizing the little bell rope by the side of the bed, he tugged it violently. In response to the summons one of his squires appeared.

The Wooden Wall.

"WHAT'S the time?" roared the Baron. " Twelve o'clock, sire," replied the squire.

" I know that, dolt !" roared the Baron. " But is it twelve o'clock at night or twelve o'clock in the morning?"

" None of us know, sire," said the squire in a frightened sort of voice. " Some of us think it is twelve o'clock in the morning. But it can't be, because it is still dark outside."

" Perhaps it's an eclipse of the sun," said the Baron. " That makes everything dark, you know."

" There is no eclipse of the sun due this year, sire," said the squire in a more frightened voice than ever. " I—I think something's happened. I think the sun must have gone out altogether or else hasn't risen at all this morning."

" Stuff and nonsense !" roared the Baron, beginning to scramble into his clothes. " We'll go and see what they make of it at the Royal Palace. Tell my men to mount their horses and to carry lanterns with them !"

A few minutes later, with tiny lanterns hung at their saddles, he and his robber band rode out of the courtyard. Next moment, however, they got the shock of their lives, for they found their way barred by a great wooden wall.

This wooden wall was the inner side of Gulliver's upturned box, of course. But the terrified Baron and his men knew nothing about that. All they knew was that their way was barred by a wooden wall which towered up and up into the darkness higher than the light of their lanterns could reach.

A quick tour brought the horrifying discovery that the castle was absolutely hemmed in by four of these mysterious wooden walls.

"We must hack our way out!" roared the Baron, nearly sick with fright. "Bring axes and we'll hack our way through one of these walls."

Gold for the Peasant.

GULLIVER, sitting outside on the upturned box, chuckled to himself as he heard the thud, thud of the tiny axes. At length a hole had been cut in the side of the box, and Baron Bawler popped his head out.

As he did so he got the shock of his life. For he felt himself seized by a giant finger and thumb and snatched up into the air.

Nor could any of his men get out through the hole in the side of the box because Gulliver had clapped his heel against it, blocking the way.

"Well, you nasty little fellow," said Gulliver to the terrified, struggling Baron. "You've had a fright this time, eh? Now you listen to me. I'm going to push you back through the hole you've just cut in the side of this big box. You'll go into your castle and bring me a bag of gold for the poor peasant woman whose cottage you burned. You'll also promise to stop your wickedness. If you don't, I shall keep you and your men prisoners inside this upturned box until you do promise!"

The Baron promised, of course. He was so terrified that he would have promised anything. He brought Gulliver the little bag of gold. Then he promised on his word of honour that he and his band would give up their wicked ways.

"Well, mind you do," warned Gulliver, picking up the box and letting daylight flood over the castle again. "If you break your promise I will punish you severely; so remember that!"

Picture excerpt taken from 'The Master Gangster of Dismal Swamp', The Skipper Book for Boys, 1948.

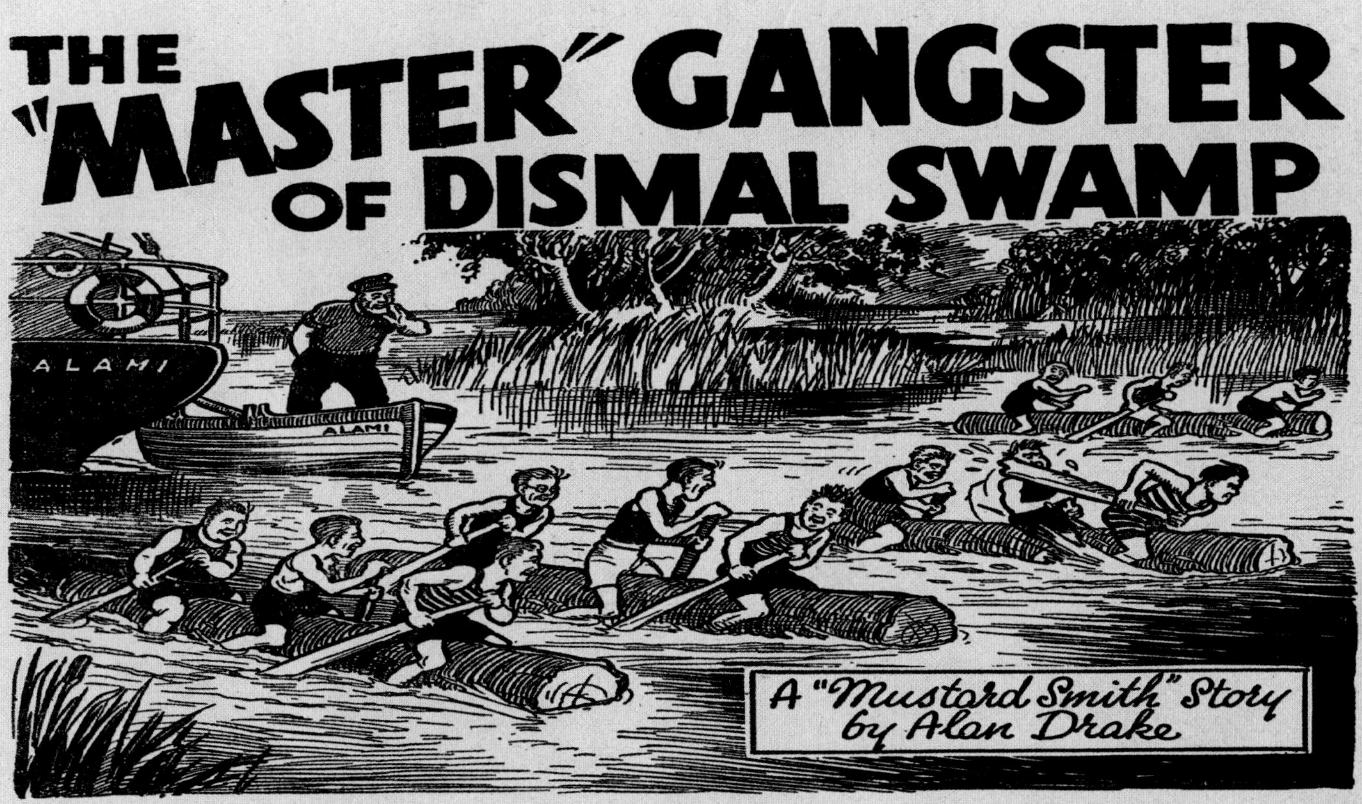

1950s

A hugely illustrious decade for Watkins, the baby boom of the 1950s brought with it a greater need for humour comics for kids, as DC Thomson launched both Beezer in 1956 and The Topper in 1953. The former debuted a new character created by Watkins called Ginger — a standard English speaking equivalent to his popular Oor Wullie. The Topper, likewise, introduced a new distinctly Dudley D cover star in its first issue, Mickey the Monkey. Watkins would be widely known for both characters, who were fan favourites among comic readers. These would be the final two characters Watkins created for DC Thomson.

However, outside of the publishing company, Watkins was known for his involvement in the community. As well as providing artwork for mission calendars in 1956, Watkins kindly donated biblical comic strips he had drawn titled William the Warrior and Tony & Tina — The Twins.

GINGER

In 1956, DC Thomson launched a new humour comic named Beezer. The new paper had a cover star drawn in the recognisable style of one Dudley D Watkins. Watkins was tasked with creating this new character, which in some ways was based on Watkins' Oor Wullie — but the new boy was named Ginger, for his obvious tuft of red hair.

However, unlike Oor Wullie, Ginger was not a general rabble-rouser or a mischief-maker. Instead, trouble often found him when he was trying to simply get by and do what most young boys want to do — play with his friends.

In his first appearance, Ginger just wants to keep warm in the winter but manages to get himself into a bunch of odd circumstances ranging from making a horse's teeth chatter to wearing a woman's fur coat. It always turns out okay in the end, though, as Ginger returns to bed with a few hot water bottles for good measure!

THE BEEZER

3d

EVERY TUESDAY

Water, water—EVERYWHERE!

AH – A FOUNTAIN!

TAKE THAT!

I NEVER MISS.

HA! HA! HA!
HO! HO! HO!

LATER
PLEASANT LITTLE SHOWER!

GINGER! IT'S TIME FOR YOUR BATH!
BATH!

NOT IF I CAN HELP IT.

THAT BOY'S SCARED STIFF OF WATER!

PHEW! THAT WAS A NEAR THING!

Ho! Ho! Ho! It's snowing BLUE snow!

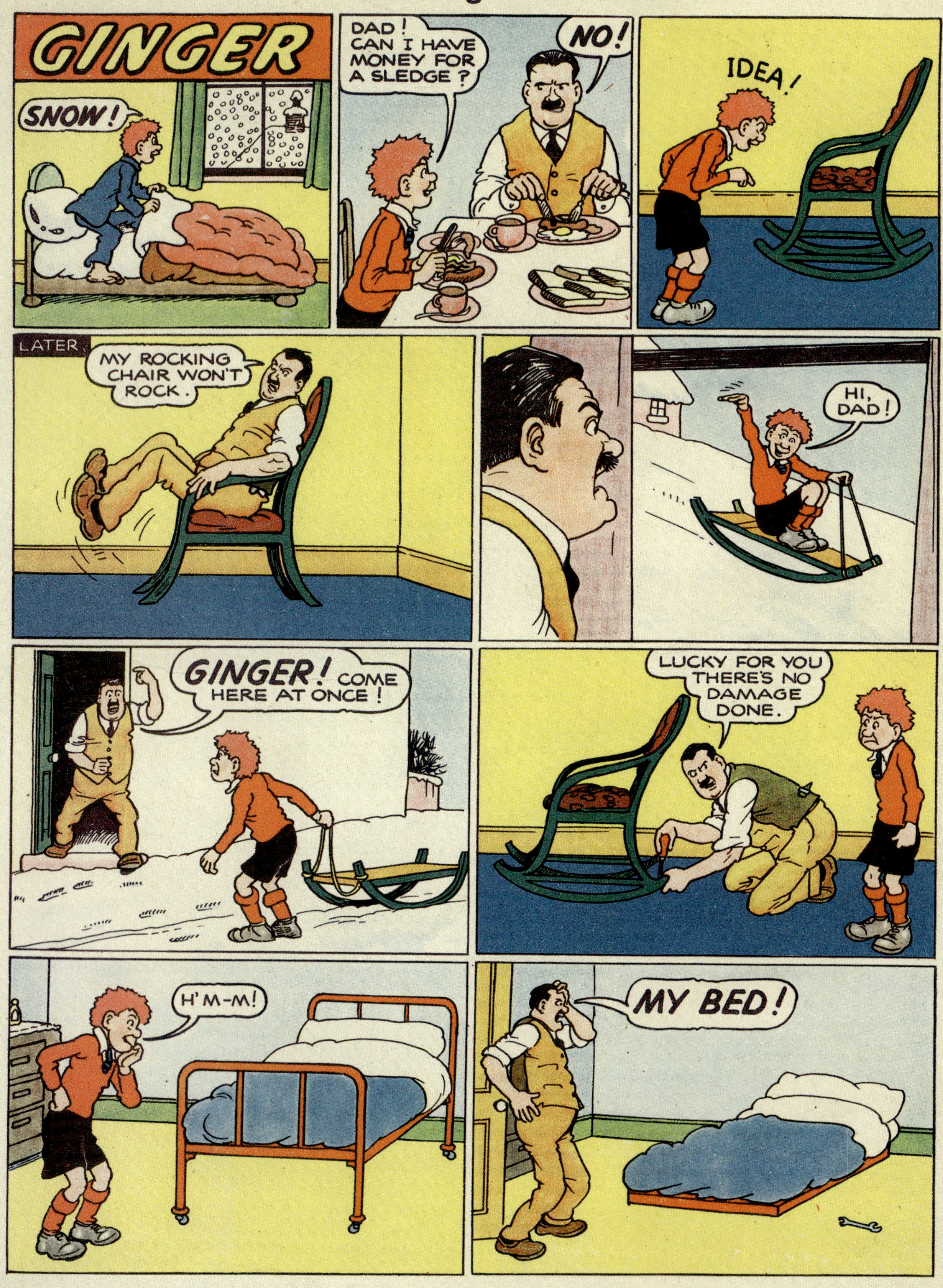

GINGER!
THIS IS GREAT!
WHY DON'T YOU BUY ME A SLEDGE, DAD?
HUH! IT'LL HAVE TO SNOW BLUE SNOW BEFORE I'LL DO THAT.
IDEA!
OH, DAD! HAVE YOU A MINUTE TO SPARE?
EH?
THERE YOU ARE..... BLUE SNOW!
????
YOU WIN.... HERE'S MONEY FOR YOUR SLEDGE.
THANKS!
HIYA, FOLKS!
HO! HO! HO! I COVERED THE WINDOW WITH THIS BLUE PAPER.

MICKEY
THE MONKEY

In 1953, a new character in dungarees entered DC Thomson's roster of strips drawn by Dudley D Watkins. Only this one wasn't called Oor Wullie and it wasn't a human boy. Instead this dungaree-wearing scamp was a monkey called Mickey.

Mickey the Monkey's first appearance was in issue No.1 of The Topper which featured the chimpanzee playing tricks on some unsuspecting guardsmen when they interrupt him playing football. The strip features no balloons, allowing Watkins' style and sense of humour to deliver more laughs. Here, you'll see Mickey's dungarees are yellow rather than his later trademark red. What's more, his parrot companion, Polly, is nowhere to be seen. These facts would be changed by Watkins over time, yellow dungarees to red, speech balloons were added, his blank white face coloured flesh tone, as well as Polly being added.

Mickey the Monkey was a regular face in The Topper and he was in every issue until the title merged with its brother comic, Beezer.

MICKEY
the
MONKEY

HA!
HA!
HA!

D. WATKINS

MICKEY the Monkey
I'M GOING OUT! BEHAVE YOURSELF!

OH, DEAR! OH, DEAR! I'VE BROKEN MICKEY'S MIRROR!
CRASH!

I'LL HANG IT UP AGAIN. MAYBE HE'LL NOT NOTICE IT.

MEANWHILE
KLONK!
DANGER
BUILDING IN PROGRESS
CEMENT

OOH! MY POOR HEAD!
MICKEY'S HOUSE

GOSH! MY HEAD'S FLATTENED!

AT THE DOC'S
DON'T BE SILLY, MICKEY, YOUR HEAD'S ALL RIGHT.
PILLS

BACK HOME
HO! HO! HA! HA! HE! HE!

LATER
I'LL TEACH POLLY A LESSON. I'VE TAKEN ALL THE GLASS OUT!
ZZZZZ

I'M FED UP WITH YOUR TRICKS. I'M GOING TO MAKE YOU VANISH!
HO! HO! YOU CAN'T KID ME!

I HAVE VANISHED!

??? HOW?? WHY ???
NOW I'LL GET SOME PEACE!

MICKEY THE Monkey
POSTMAN! POSTMAN!

PANT~ PUFF~ JUST IN TIME!
CLICK

THANK YOU!
I'LL TAKE IT!

AND POP IT IN THE PILLAR BOX~ IT'LL GO WITH THE NEXT COLLECTION.

BALLOONS
I'LL FIX HIM!

HELP!
WHIZZ
HA- HA- HA!
D. WATKINS

1. Trouble for Snooty ! There was a Pet Show on down town and he hadn't entered so much as a pedigree tadpole ! But Lord Sniffington, who lived in the castle next door, had. And when Aunt Mat saw Lord Sniffington marching with his pets she looked huffy and snapped, " Lord Snooty, get cracking !" or words to that effect. The only pets Snooty had were Polly Wolly Doodle's poodle and Contrary Mary the Mule and they both badly needed haircuts.

2. The two animals had put up with a lot since they'd joined Lord Snooty's Gang, but the worst was yet to come ! In two ticks they were having their hair cut and not just an ordinary back and sides either. Snooty had decided to enter his pets as French poodles or nothing ! And like nothing they were when the scissors stopped clicking—like nothing on earth ! They looked as if the moths had been at them. Scrapper shouldn't have let them see themselves in the mirror !

3. The panicky pets fairly goggled at themselves in the looking glass, and groaned. A blind-folded man using a fork and knife could have cut their hair better. "They're just bashful 'cause we've made them look so handsome," said Scrapper. "Maybe when we've won all the prizes at the Pet Show with them we could get them a film contract!" But the mule and the poodle weren't bashful. They were full of bash! Wham! They lashed out and sent the Gang sprawling in a heap.

4. Pongo and Mary were off down the road, like peas from a peashooter, to repair the damage to themselves. Ting-a-ling! The bell above the hairdresser's door rang like a fire alarm as they flashed inside. The barber prided himself on his lightning hair restorer, and the mule and the poodle certainly needed a basinful. In two shakes of a cat's tail they had used up three bottles of the stuff. The barber bellowed and pulled Mary's tail, but he couldn't stop the pets.

5. When the mule and the poodle finally charged out of the shop, Pongo was the shaggiest dog in Britain and Mary had a fur coat to make a duchess green with envy. They certainly looked handsome enough for the Pet Show now. But they weren't going to enter. They knocked Snooty and his pals out of the way like ninepins and scampered off to parade themselves around town. Snooty was furious. "That's what we get for trying to make them famous!" he raged.

6. Still, Snooty was the boy for bright ideas, even if they didn't often work out. "Hooray!" As he was passing a shop which sold animal skins, he gave a cheer that nearly lifted his top hat into the air. There was a crocodile skin and a gorilla skin for sale. "There are our new pets!" he cried. "I know how to win the Pet Show prizes now." So the Gang sorted out the buttons from their spare coppers, scraped the old toffee off the money and bought the skins.

7. Soon Big Fat Joe was inside the gorilla skin. He was just the right fit through eating two double helpings at dinner-time every day, except Sunday when he ate four. It wasn't so easy making a crocodile out of Scrapper, but Snooty did make him weep crocodile tears by sticking a needle in the poor chap while he was stitching the skin up. They were finished just in time. Lord Sniffington had already gone strutting into the Pet Show with his entries.

8. Galloping grasshoppers! No one ever had exhibited an ape or a crocodile at Bunkerton Pet Show before. When Snooty entered with his fierce-looking pets pandemonium broke out. The judge climbed the pole, and Lord Sniffington and his pals headed for home through the nearest emergency exit. "That's not a thoroughbred gorilla," gulped Sniffy as he bolted. "I can't show my pets in the same show as it." But he was really shaking so much his socks nearly fell off.

9.   Soon, apart from the judge and a few pets in their boxes, Snooty and his pals were alone in the Pet Show. The judge didn't want to come down from the pole in case Snooty's pets thought he was the first prize and carried him off. So he told Snooty he'd won all the cups! "Hooray!" whooped Snooty. "Aunt Mat will double our pocket money." But two jealous faces were peeping into the marquee. Pongo and Mary had come to see the fun and they didn't like it!

10.   "We're not having gorillas or crocodiles in the same gang as us," they thought. "Next thing we know Snooty will be bringing elephants in. Then we'll get nothing to eat." Determined to settle accounts with the two new pets straightaway, Pongo and Mary launched a surprise attack from the doorway. With two well-placed kicks, Mary sent the gorilla that was really Big Fat Joe crashing against the tent-pole, while Pongo bit the crocodile that was really Scrapper.

11. Scrapper and Joe would have leapt out of the fake skins and shown their pets they had nothing to be jealous about. But the pole Joe had cracked with his head was the one that held the marquee up. In two split half-seconds the canvas came down and everyone but the judge, who was still up the other pole, was sent sprawling. When the Gang threw the canvas aside the judge saw Scrapper and Joe crawling out of the animal skins. "Tricked!" he muttered.

12. Trouble, trouble, trouble! Swanky's nose needed splinting. Snatch and Snitch each had black eyes. Scrapper was on crutches, Joe was in bandages and Polly was in tears. Doubting Thomas thought he had a broken jaw and Snooty didn't just think he had something—he knew he had. Instead of the jangling of silver cups as Snooty handed them over, all Aunt Mat heard was the rustling of paper. The only prize Snooty got was the bill for the damages at the Pet Show.

DESPERATE DAN

DAN'S "DIVE" TAKES HIM HIGHER AND HIGHER,
UNTIL HE'S A REAL SKY-HIGH FLIER.
BUT LATER HE'S FOUND DEEP DOWN UNDERGROUND,
AND SO RICH THAT HE NOW CAN RETIRE.
OH, DEAR. I HAVEN'T LANDED QUITE RIGHT.

I'M BOUNCING TOO HIGH THIS TIME.

WOW! THROUGH THE ROOF!
SWIMMING BATHS

CRASH
RIGHT INTO A PESKY PLANE. WHAT TOUGH LUCK!

THAT'S TORN IT!

I'LL GLIDE BACK DOWN TO EARTH NOW.
LOOK OUT, DAN. YOU'RE TANGLING MY PARACHUTE

DON'T WORRY. WE'LL MAKE A HAPPY LANDING.

BACK AT THE BATHS
HUH! THIS ISN'T VERY HAPPY!
SWIMMING BATHS

A FINE DIVE THAT WAS!

A FINE MESS! OUR CLOTHES RUINED! WE'LL SUE YOU!

HEY, DAN! YOU'D BETTER STAY DOWN OUT OF SIGHT. THERE'S A LOAD OF TROUBLE UP HERE.

SWOOSH

I COULDN'T STAY DOWN. YOU'RE IN LUCK. I'VE STRUCK OIL!

SIX WEEKS LATER
I'M PESKY GLAD I MET YOU, PARTNER. IMAGINE HAVING AN OIL WELL NOW INSTEAD OF A SWIMMING BATH!
SWIMMING BATHS
OIL WELLS
D. WATKINS

BIFFO
THE BEAR
LOOK, BIFFO! A BABY RHINO'S ESCAPING FROM THE ZOO.
ZOO
STALE BUNS GOING CHEAP 6 A PENNY
GIVE ME SIX PENNYWORTH, PLEASE.
SNORE
RHINO'S ASLEEP. NOW'S MY CHANCE TO LAY A TRAIL OF BUNS.
MUNCH
OLD VILLAGE STOCKS AS USED IN THE 16TH CENTURY
BIFFO'S HOOPLA 12 SHOTS FOR A ½ D
Q HERE
D. WATKINS

BIFFO the BEAR

DESPERATE DAN

I MUST LEARN TO BOWL STRAIGHT FOR THE CRICKET MATCH ON SATURDAY.

THAT BALL BROKE TO BITS. I'LL HAVE TO TRY A CANNON BALL.

WHERE IS IT?

TEN MINUTES LATER
AH! GOT IT AT LAST!

WHERE DID THAT ONE GO?

I SEE — RIGHT THROUGH THE FENCE!
— AND YOU'RE PLAYING AGAINST US TOMORROW.
OH, GOSH!

NOW I CAN BOWL STRAIGHT!
I MUST TELL THE OTHER PLAYERS!

NEXT DAY
D. WATKINS

DESPERATE DAN

YOU KNOW WHO'S COMING ? THE MAN WITH THE FUNNIEST FACE IN THE WILD WEST !
YOU DON'T MEAN — ?
TURNING PALE !

YES ! DESPERATE DAN !
ANY GRUB IN THIS TOWN ?
IT'S DAN !

DON'T STAY HERE, DAN. THE GRUB'S POISONOUS !
I'LL RISK IT. I'M STARVING !

WE MUST GET RID OF HIM SOMEHOW. LET'S MAKE HIS DINNER HORRID. BRING SOME MORE FURNITURE POLISH !
HURRY UP THERE !
CYCLE OIL
DOG BISCUITS
TACKS
SHOT FOR GUNS

YUM-YUM ! THIS IS TASTY ! DELICIOUS ! I LIKE THESE LITTLE HARD CURRANTS IN IT TOO !
WHISPER— THE 'CURRANTS' ARE LEAD SHOT ! IT'S NO GOOD, WE'LL HAVE TO KNOCK HIM OUT TILL THE SHOW IS OVER !

HERE GOES !
YUM-YUM ! LOVELY COFFEE !
THOUGHT— LOVELY COFFEE INDEED ! WHY, WE PUT BROWN BOOT POLISH IN IT !

HELP ! HIS HEAD'S GONE RIGHT THROUGH THE BOTTOM OF THE POT !
YOU HAVEN'T KNOCKED HIM OUT, LUKE—BUT HE'S BLINDFOLDED NOW ! COME ON, IT'S TIME FOR THE CONTEST

NOW WHERE DID THOSE GUYS GO ? WHAT'S ALL THE MYSTERY ?
HA HA HA

IT'LL BE BEHIND THAT FENCE—I'LL LOOK THROUGH THAT VACANT HOLE ON GROUND LEVEL !
HA ! HA ! HA ! HA ! HA
TURN OVER AND SEE THE SURPRISE DAN GOT

WOW! WHAT'S HAPPENED?
OOOO! I'M SPIFFLICATED!
YOU'VE BUST MY BRACES, MAN! I'LL- I'LL COURT MARTIAL YOU!
HI! WHAT'S THE PESKY GAME?
N-N-NEIGH! HIC- NEIGH!
DRAT IT I KNEW DAN WOULD BEAT ALL AT THIS CONTEST
OUCH!
HELP! MY 80-YEAR-OLD WHISKERS! THIS FENCE IS PULLING THEM OFF!
DAN HAS HAD TO HOIST UP THE WHOLE FENCE TO SEE WHAT'S GOING ON!
DEADPAN CITY

GROAN
OF ALL THE CHEEK! I DON'T NEED MY FACE LIFTED!
GET ME DOWN! I'VE SWALLOWED MY BACK TEETH!
THEY'RE NOT YOUR KIDNEYS - THEY'RE MINE!
HOI! SHIFT YOUR FACE FUNGUS! NOBODY CAN SEE HOW FUNNY I LOOK!
YOU UP THERE! GET YOUR KNEES OUT OF MY KIDNEYS.
YOU'RE DEAD RIGHT, LUKE. YOU DIDN'T HIT HIM HARD ENOUGH!
I'LL NEVER MAKE A FUNNY FACE AGAIN!
HAVE A HEART, DAN. I CAME HERE TO SHOW MY FACE - NOT TO GET MY HEAD PULLED OFF!
HA-HA! LOOK AT DAN'S FACE! YOU WIN THE PRIZE, DAN!
FUNNY FACE CONTEST
1st PRIZE
CASH
NOW THERE'S STRENGTH FOR YOU! SEVENTEEN PEOPLE AND A HORSE LIFTED CLEAN OFF THEIR FEET!
D. WATKINS

THE TRICKS OF TOM THUMB

TOM THUMB, the smallest boy in the world, was having a grand time on Farmer Digson's farm. A catapult was stuck upright in the ground and the sling of the catapult made an ideal swing for wee Tom, who was only six inches tall. To and fro he swung all afternoon, until heavy footsteps sounded on the path and a loud voice shouted, "Of all the cheek!" It was Oliver Jenks, a boy who worked on the farm.

With a flick of their tails the rabbits that were watching Tom scampered off into the forest as Oliver Jenks reached down and grabbed hold of Tom in one hand. "That's my catapult!" said Jenks, as he lifted Tom into the air. "And if you want to play with it, you ask me first." Poor Tom squirmed helplessly in the grip of the boy's strong fingers. "Let me down, you big bully," he gasped. But Oliver Jenks only laughed.

"That's not what my catapult's for anyway," said the burly Oliver, with a grin on his face, as he fitted Tom into the sling and began to draw back on the elastic. "This is how it works." And before Tom knew what was happening, Jenks released the sling. T-w-a-aaa-ang! Poor Tom went whizzing through the air so fast he thought the end of the world had come. Over and over and over he tumbled in the air.

The farmer's boy had aimed the catapult at a nearby duckpond, and Tom had a glimpse of the water far below him. Then down he came, holding his breath for the big splash. As luck would have it, an old boot was floating on the surface of the pond, and Tom landed right inside it and lay there until he got his breath back. He could hear the water lapping against the uppers of the floating boot.

Quack-Quack! The noisy ducks quickly brought Tommy to his feet, and he groaned when he found that he was stranded right in the middle of the duckpond. To little Tom the water seemed to stretch for miles around. Then Tom had a bright idea when he saw the lace attached to the boot. He quickly made a noose in the bootlace and cleverly lassoed the head of a duck that was turning to swim away across the pond.

"I'll soon reach the edge of the pond now," gasped Tom, as the duck set off, pulling the boot through the water at a great rate. But Oliver Jenks was standing on the bank watching Tom, and he hadn't finished being nasty. "I'll make him swim for it," the bully muttered. He picked up a stone and hurled it into the water, raising a splash that almost drowned poor Tom and caused him to lose hold of the bootlace.

The boot capsized and Tom fell into the water, and Oliver Jenks roared with laughter as he walked off towards the farm to finish his day's work. "The - big - bully!" spluttered Tom, as he struck out for the shore, expecting every minute to be snapped up by an angry duck. Poor Tom was glad to stumble safely ashore through the muddy shallows and he collapsed exhausted on the bank.

The hot sun dried Tom's clothes as he squelched up the road towards the farm. Although he was the smallest boy in the world, Tom had the heart of a lion—and he meant to get his revenge on Oliver Jenks. Half an hour later Tom was perched on a farm gate when he saw Oliver driving a pair of horses down the road towards him. At once little Tom Thumb thought of a way of getting his own back on the approaching bully.

The farmer's boy was smirking all over his oily fat face, and standing with his feet astride the horses—one foot on Dobbin, the other on Dick. Clippity-clop! Clippity-clop! The horses approached the farm gate at a fast trot. Oliver was so cocky and sure of himself that he failed to see the tiny figure of Tom leap out from the gate and snatch hold of Dobbin's rein as the horses cantered smartly past into the field beyond.

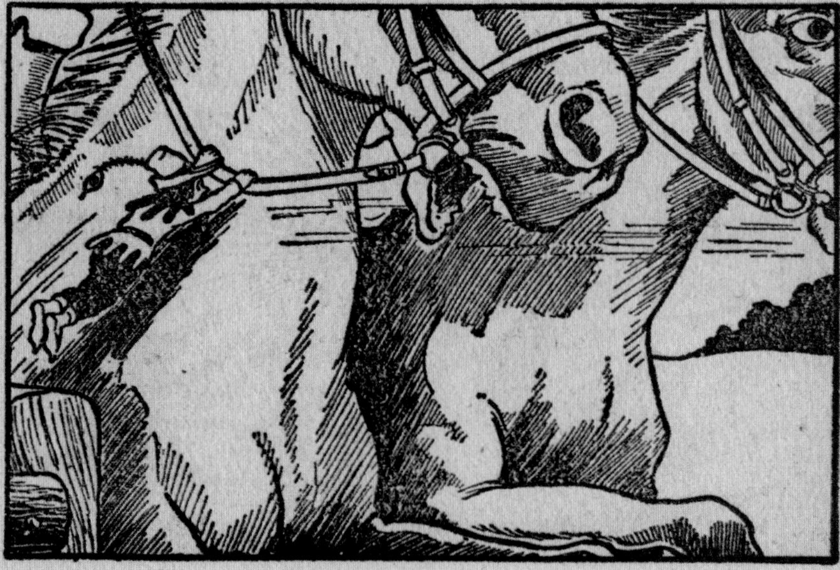

Tom was taking a big risk as he clung to Dobbin's rein. One slip and he would fall beneath the thundering hoofs. But Tom was out to get his own back on Oliver. He tightened his hold and braced his tiny feet against Dobbin's head. "I'll get even with that bully!" he panted, as he strained hard at the reins, in an effort to pull Dobbin's head round. "Round this way, Dobbin!" he gasped, heaving with all his strength.

The horses were swiftly approaching a trough in the field, and Oliver was carelessly guiding the horses to pass on one side of it. But he reckoned without Tom Thumb, whose pull on the reins sent Dobbin galloping suddenly down one side of the trough, while Dick went down the other side. "Hi! Whoa there, Dobbin!" yelled Oliver in a panic as he saw Dobbin turn away. The bully saw what was coming—too late!

The horses drew apart, Oliver lost his footing, and with a mighty splash he landed flat on his back in the flooded trough. Tom nearly split his sides laughing as he cantered round the field, holding on to Dobbin's ears. "That should teach the bully a lesson," he gurgled, as he watched Oliver squelch off home. "He won't be so keen to play dirty tricks on me in future. Ho-ho-ho!"

BIFFO THE BEAR
I'LL FOOL BIFFO WITH THESE SPECIAL SUCTION SHOES! I CAN WALK ANYWHERE WITH THEM.

HO! HO! I FEEL JUST LIKE A FLY! NOTHING LIKE THE WIDE OPEN SPACES FOR HAVING FUN —
IT'S BUSTER!?

— NOBODY CAN GET AT YOU!
BIFFO

HIYA, BIFFO!
OUCH!

I JUMPED UP IN TIME!

LOOK! I'M WALKING ROUND YOUR KITCHEN WALLS.
IDEA!

I'LL OPEN THE WINDOW!

HELP!
BRRR
WHAT? LEAVING SO SOON, BUSTER?

RUBBISH CART
HA! HA! THAT WAS ONE WIDE-OPEN SPACE HE DIDN'T LIKE!

BIFFO
THE BEAR

IT'S STARTING TO RAIN!

DO YOU MIND IF I SHELTER UNDER YOUR GAMP?

YES! I DO MIND ~ GET OUT OF MY WAY!
OUCH!

THOUGHT — I'LL NIP IN BEHIND HIM.

OH, NO, YOU DON'T! BUY AN UMBRELLA FOR YOURSELF.
GARAGE

GARAGE
FREE AIR
THOUGHT — I'LL BLOW SOME OF THIS FREE AIR INTO HIS GAMP
OH, GOSH! THE WIND'S GETTING UP! WHAT A SUDDEN STORM!

FREE AIR
HISS

DESPERATE DAN

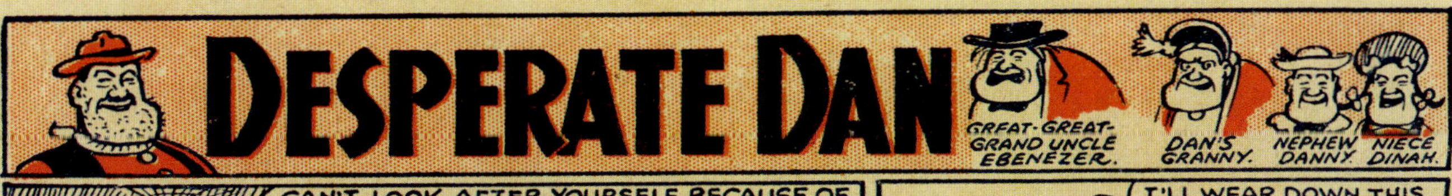

DESPERATE DAN
GREAT-GREAT-GRAND UNCLE EBENEZER.
DAN'S GRANNY.
NEPHEW DANNY.
NIECE DINAH.

CAN'T LOOK AFTER YOURSELF BECAUSE OF YOUR RHEUMATICS, UNCLE EB?~ DON'T WORRY~WE'LL SOON CURE YOU.
HUH! UNCLE EB IS 156 YEARS OLD, AND HE LOOKS YOUNGER EVERY DAY.

I'LL WEAR DOWN THIS IRON FILE AGAINST MY CHIN TO MAKE IRON TONIC FOR POOR OLD UNCLE EB.
I'LL STIR IT UP.

THAT'S THE IRON TONIC MIXED UP I'LL POUR IT INTO THIS BOTTLE.
WE'RE GOING SWIMMING TO CATCH A SHARK!
GURGLE
FILE

WE WANT SOME SHARK'S LIVER OIL FOR UNCLE EB'S RHEUMATICS. HERE'S ONE!

POP IT THROUGH THE MANGLE AND SQUEEZE OUT THE LIVER OIL!
UNCLE EB NEEDS BEAR GREASE, TOO!

SKIPPING AND WEIGHT-LIFTING IS MAKING THEM SWEAT BEAR GREASE THROUGH THE IRON RAILINGS INTO THE BUCKETS!

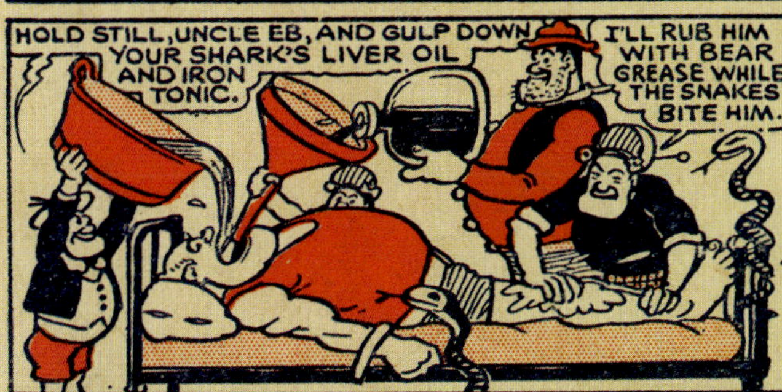

HOLD STILL, UNCLE EB, AND GULP DOWN YOUR SHARK'S LIVER OIL AND IRON TONIC.
I'LL RUB HIM WITH BEAR GREASE WHILE THE SNAKES BITE HIM.

AN HOUR LATER
HA·HA! EBENEZER IS SO FIT, HE CAN JUGGLE DANNY AND DINAH AND DANCE A JIG AT THE SAME TIME.

I'M CURED! COME ON, YOU LAZY LUBBERS! CLEAN UP MY HOUSE, CUT THE GRASS AND WASH THE DISHES, OR I'LL BIFF YOU ALL!
HUH! WE GOT UNCLE EB BETTER SO THAT HE COULD LOOK AFTER HIMSELF, BUT NOW HE'S MAKING US DO EVERYTHING INSTEAD~ AND HE'S TOO OLD AND TOUGH TO ARGUE WITH.
D. WATKINS

BIFFO AND BUSTER

BIFFO THE BEAR

1960s

The sixties continued to be a boom time for comic illustrators, and Watkins worked on a huge array of weekly comics, Christmas Specials and Summer Specials across DC Thomson's catalogue. He still found time to pursue other interests outside of his work, supporting the local church he was a member of.

During the final decade of his life, Watkins illustrated two full-colour biblical strips that appeared in The Sparky annuals in 1968 and 1969. His ultimate ambition was to adapt the Bible into a similar format, but sadly, he never managed to fulfil this dream.

LORD SNOOTY AND HIS PALS
LORD MARMADUKE— "SNOOTY" TO YOU!
ROSIE.
HAIRPIN HUGGINS.
SKINNY LIZZIE.
SCRAPPER SMITH.
"HAPPY" HUTTON.
GERTIE THE GOAT.

THAT'S A NICE DOLL'S HOUSE, ROSIE.

MY DOLL'S HOUSE IS MUCH GRANDER THAN ROSIE'S!
WOW! SO IT IS, LIZ!

AND LOOK INSIDE—
—REAL ANTIQUE DOLL'S FURNITURE!

WELL, I'M GLAD SHE'S GONE. I'LL PLAY WITH MY DOLL'S TEA-SET NOW.

IT'S NOT REAL TEA, OF COURSE— JUST LEMONADE.
WHY, THAT'S SUPER, ROSIE!

JUST WAIT TILL YOU SEE MY TEA-SET, THOUGH!
HIGH TEA SET

THIS IS A POSH TEA-SET, EH?

AND HERE'S MY NEW WALKIE-TALKIE DOLL.

IT CAN BOTH SPEAK AND WALK.
I'M FED UP OF LIZ'S BOASTING!
MAMA!
WHIRR!

SHORTLY—
NOW I'D LIKE YOU TO SEE MY NEW WALKIE-TALKIE DOLLS.

HERE THEY ARE!
THEY CAN WALK ALL RIGHT, BUT CAN THEY TALK?

MUMMY! WE WANT A DRINK OF WATER, AND WILL YOU READ A STORY TO US, PLEASE?
GASP!

HUMPH! I MUST SAY THEY'RE VERY LIFE-LIKE!
ENVY
PROD

THEY'RE LIFE-LIKE ALL RIGHT! ONE'S BITTEN HER FINGER AND THE OTHER'S PULLED HER HAIR! HO! HO! HO!
EEK!
GNASH!
TUG

HA! HA! IT'S ONLY SNITCH AND SNATCH DRESSED UP!
THAT'S WHAT YOU GET FOR BRAGGING SO MUCH!

LORD SNOOTY AND HIS PALS
LORD MARMADUKE— "SNOOTY" TO YOU!
ROSIE.
HAIRPIN HUGGINS.
SKINNY LIZZIE.
SCRAPPER SMITH.
"HAPPY" HUTTON.
GERTIE THE GOAT.

I'VE JUST FOUND THIS ANCIENT DOCUMENT—IT SAYS THAT IN BYGONE DAYS THE LORD OF BUNKERTON USED TO FIRE A CANNON AT ONE O'CLOCK EVERY DAY. I THINK IT MIGHT BE A GOOD IDEA TO REVIVE THE CUSTOM.
OK, MR MAYOR!
SHORTLY—
HERE'S THE OLD CANNON— COVERED IN DUST.
NOW WE'VE GOT IT OUT IN THE OPEN WE CAN GIVE IT A GOOD POLISH.
LATER—
THE CANNON'S READY WHENEVER THE MAYOR IS.
EVERY DAY AT ONE, FROM NOW AND FOR EVER, THE CANNON WILL FIRE. NOW, SNOOTY!
BOOM!
CRUMBS! WE FORGOT TO CLEAN THE INSIDE OF THE CANNON!
COUGH
NEXT DAY—
READY TO FIRE AGAIN!
THE MAYOR HAS STAYED AT HOME TODAY!
BOOM!
AT THE MAYOR'S—
SHATTER!
BOOM!
CRASH!
GRR! THE NOISE HAS BLOWN MY WINDOWS IN!
SO—
CAN YOU MAKE OUR CANNON SAFE, PROFESSOR SCREWTOP?
AHEM!—LET ME SEE...
NEXT DAY—
IT SHOULD BE SAFE NOW!
?!?

HA! HA! WELL DONE, PROFESSOR!
CUCKOO!
POP!

SNOOTY'S CUCKOO GUN IS BANG ON TIME!
DON'T MENTION BANGS TO ME!
MAYOR
TICK! TICK!

DESPERATE DAN

BOWLING GREEN

THERE GO SOME YOUNG LADS OFF TO PLAY CRICKET! I WOULDN'T MIND A GAME MYSELF!

HIYA, DAN!

BOWLING GREEN

YOU IDIOT!

AH! A CRICKET BALL FROM SOME-WHERE!

HMM! THEY MUST BE MAKING CRICKET BALLS BIGGER NOWADAYS! THIS ONE JUST FITS MY HAND NICELY

STOP! STOP! THAT'S MY BOWL!

BOWL! I THOUGHT IT WAS A CRICKET BALL AND I'M AIMING AT THAT TREE AS A WICKET!

OH! TOO LATE!

SORRY, MISTER! IT'S GONE RIGHT THROUGH THE TREE!

HUH! THAT TREE MUST BE ROTTEN IN THE MIDDLE!

I'M NOT SO SURE IT'S ROTTEN! IT'S FLATTENED MY BOWL!

TOO BAD. BUT. I'VE PROVED I'M STILL FAIRLY GOOD AT CRICKET! I MUST GET A GAME!

THAT BATSMAN'S HIT IT FOR SIX! AND THE FIELDER WILL NEVER CATCH IT— UNLESS I HELP HIM!

UP YOU GO! CATCH IT!

WOW! WHAT'S HAPPENING?

CLAP

DRAT IT! I'VE MISSED IT!

BAH! IT'S SLIPPED THROUGH HIS FINGERS!

CAUGHT THEM BOTH!

OUT!

I SAY, DAN. OUR TEAM'S A MAN SHORT, SO HERE'S YOUR CHANCE TO BAT. BUT WATCH THE BOWLER—HE'S MIGHTY FAST—

THANKS! LEAVE THE BOWLER TO ME!

HERE COMES THE FAST BOWLER NOW—

I MUST HAVE SENT IT FOR SIX!

YOU MUTT! WHAT A MISS!

BUT IT WASN'T A MISS! I HIT THAT BALL MIGHTY HARD!

—AND THERE'S THE PROOF! LOOK!

MY BAT!

CAPTAIN

WELL, I RECKON I'M STILL SOME GOOD AT CRICKET BUT I CAN'T GET A GAME BECAUSE BATS AND BALLS AREN'T AS STRONG AS THEY USED TO BE!

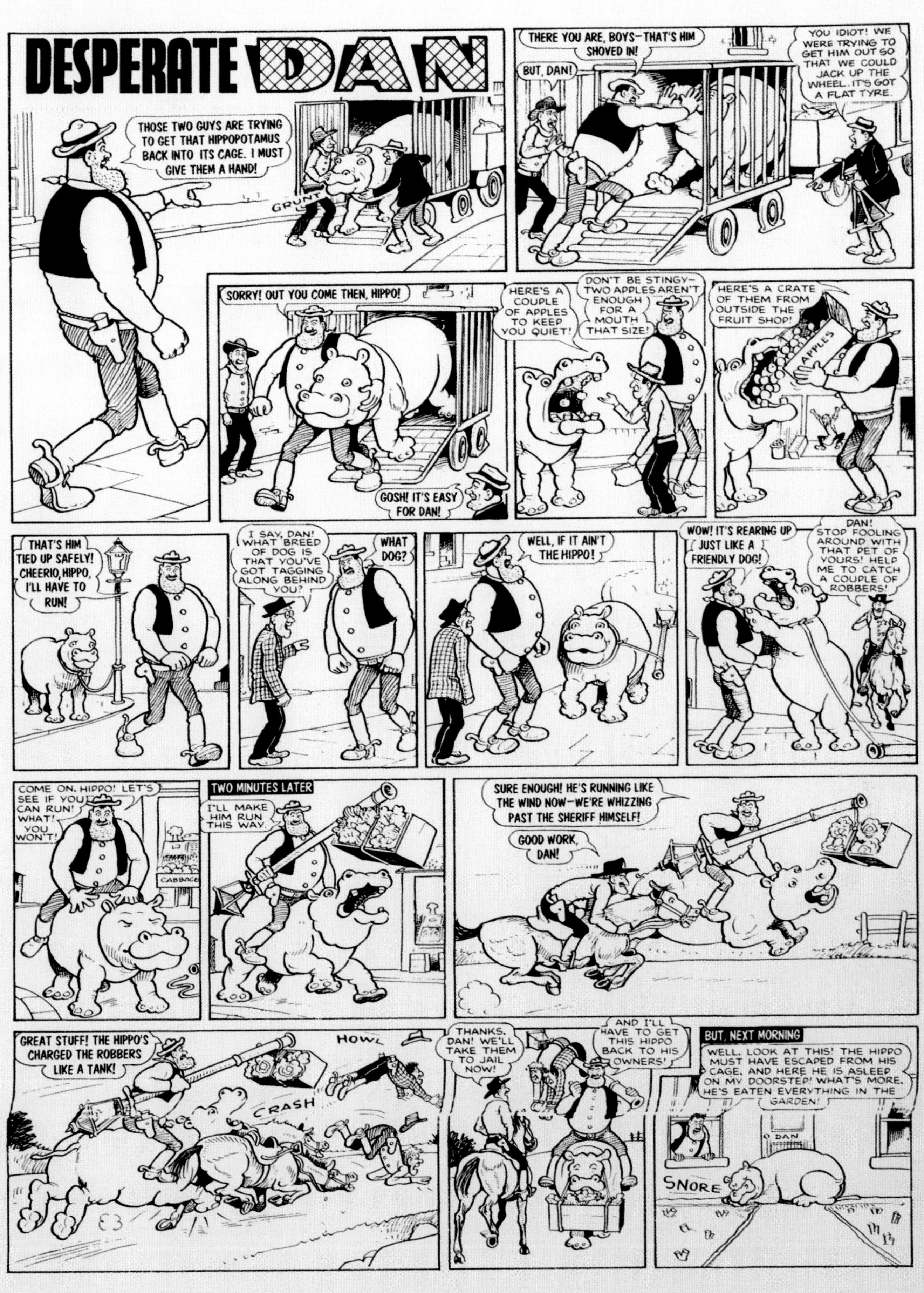

DESPERATE DAN

THOSE TWO GUYS ARE TRYING TO GET THAT HIPPOPOTAMUS BACK INTO ITS CAGE. I MUST GIVE THEM A HAND!
GRUNT

THERE YOU ARE, BOYS—THAT'S HIM SHOVED IN!
BUT, DAN!
YOU IDIOT! WE WERE TRYING TO GET HIM OUT SO THAT WE COULD JACK UP THE WHEEL. IT'S GOT A FLAT TYRE.

SORRY! OUT YOU COME THEN, HIPPO!
GOSH! IT'S EASY FOR DAN!
HERE'S A COUPLE OF APPLES TO KEEP YOU QUIET!
DON'T BE STINGY—TWO APPLES AREN'T ENOUGH FOR A MOUTH THAT SIZE!
HERE'S A CRATE OF THEM FROM OUTSIDE THE FRUIT SHOP!
APPLES

THAT'S HIM TIED UP SAFELY! CHEERIO, HIPPO, I'LL HAVE TO RUN!
I SAY, DAN! WHAT BREED OF DOG IS THAT YOU'VE GOT TAGGING ALONG BEHIND YOU?
WHAT DOG?
WELL, IF IT AIN'T THE HIPPO!
WOW! IT'S REARING UP JUST LIKE A FRIENDLY DOG!
DAN! STOP FOOLING AROUND WITH THAT PET OF YOURS! HELP ME TO CATCH A COUPLE OF ROBBERS!

COME ON, HIPPO! LET'S SEE IF YOU CAN RUN! WHAT! YOU WON'T!
CABBAGE
TWO MINUTES LATER
I'LL MAKE HIM RUN THIS WAY.
SURE ENOUGH! HE'S RUNNING LIKE THE WIND NOW—WE'RE WHIZZING PAST THE SHERIFF HIMSELF!
GOOD WORK, DAN!

GREAT STUFF! THE HIPPO'S CHARGED THE ROBBERS LIKE A TANK!
HOWL
CRASH
THANKS, DAN! WE'LL TAKE THEM TO JAIL NOW!
AND I'LL HAVE TO GET THIS HIPPO BACK TO HIS OWNERS!
BUT, NEXT MORNING
WELL, LOOK AT THIS! THE HIPPO MUST HAVE ESCAPED FROM HIS CAGE, AND HERE HE IS ASLEEP ON MY DOORSTEP! WHAT'S MORE, HE'S EATEN EVERYTHING IN THE GARDEN!
DAN
SNORE

MICKEY
THE MONKEY
WHISTLE
CAUTION
OVERHEAD
REPAIRS
KEEP
CLEAR

CAUTION
OVERHEAD
REPAIRS
KEEP
CLEAR
HOI!
WHIZZ!
CRASH

WHY DON'T YOU READ THE NOTICE?
OH!
CAUTION
OVERHEAD
REPAIRS
KEEP
CLEAR

I DIDN'T SEE IT!
AH! SOMEBODY NOT BEWARING OF ME!
BEWARE OF THE DOG.

ANOTHER NOTICE I DIDN'T NOTICE!
BEWARE OF THE DOG.

I MUST DO WHAT NOTICES SAY!

PUSH...
PUSH

INSIDE
PULL...
PULL

...AND...

LIFT
HUP!

MICKEY
THE MONKEY
TO THE ZOO

PUT THESE NOTICES OUTSIDE THE CAGES, MICKEY.
ALL RIGHT.
LION
TIGER
SEAL

FIRST ONE~ THE LION!
LION

THIS IS EASY~ I KNOW ALL THE ANIMALS.
ZEBRA

AN AMUS? ER...MUST BE A NEW ANIMAL!
AMUS

WHAT ELSE IS THERE?

WHATEVER'S THAT?
OPOT

I CAN'T FIND THESE ANIMALS!
HO! HO! I'LL SHOW YOU, MICKEY!
OPOT
AMUS

OH! NOW I SEE
HIPP OPOT AMUS

THERE'S A HOLE IN ONE OF MY POCKETS, MUM!
I'M NOT SURPRISED! YOU ALWAYS HAVE FAR TOO MUCH RUBBISH IN YOUR POCKETS. EMPTY OUT THE OTHER ONE.

JUST LOOK AT THAT! IT'S RIDICULOUS! I'M PUTTING A STOP TO THIS!

LATER
THERE! I'VE SEWN THEM UP SO YOU CAN'T USE THEM. YOU'LL LOOK MUCH TIDIER NOW!
AW, MUM!

HI, GINGER! HERE'S THE CATAPULT I BORROWED!
THANKS, TOM. I WONDER WHERE I'LL PUT IT—AH! I KNOW!

HULLO, GINGER! IS THIS YOUR PEN? I FOUND IT AT SCHOOL.
OH, YES!

I OWE YOU THREE MARBLES, GINGER. HERE THEY ARE!
THANKS, BILL!

LET'S BUY SOME SWEETS, GINGER.
GOOD IDEA, PETE!

AH! HERE'S GINGER NOW! AND DOESN'T HE LOOK TIDY WITHOUT BULGING POCKETS?

GINGER!

GINGER

GOT TO PUT ON MY HOLSTER. I ALWAYS WEAR IT WHEN I EAT MY BANANA!

OH! OH! HERE COMES TOMMY!

HI, TOMMY!
HELLO, GINGER!

VERY HANDY FOR HIDING A BANANA. SAVES ME FROM SHARING IT!

BUT IN TOMMY'S HOUSE.
GINGER CAN'T FOOL ME WITH THAT OLD TRICK OF HIS!

QUICK! HIDE MY BANANA! HERE'S TOMMY AGAIN!
I'LL MAKE HIM DRAW— AND WHEN HE DOES HE'LL HAVE TO GIVE ME A BITE.

OKAY, GINGER— DRAW!

HELP! I'VE SQUEEZED IT TOO HARD!

THANKS, GINGER. I GOT EVEN MORE THAN I EXPECTED!
BAH!

MICKEY

RIGHT, POLLY. LET'S GET STARTED!

NOSE CLIP AND EAR PLUGS!

FLIPPERS!

GOGGLES!

READY WITH THE LIFEBELT?
OF COURSE!

I'LL DO A FEW EXERCISES TO AVOID CRAMP.

AH, WELL! IT'S NOW OR NEVER!

WISH ME LUCK!

OOH! HELP! AAH!
OH, BOY—

—HE'S SUCH A COWARD AT TAKING A BATH!
IT'S TOO COLD! IT'S TOO DEEP! IT'S TOO WET! I'M DROWNING! HELP!

MICKEY
THE MONKEY
DON'T WORRY, JIMMY! I'LL GET YOUR KITE!

THERE!
FUME

I'LL JUST DROP DOWN!

YEOW!
STAMP

ER... S-SORRY, OFFICER!
GRR! YOU SHOULDN'T HAVE BEEN UP THERE ANYWAY!

THAT CAT SEEMS TO BE STUCK! I'LL RESCUE IT!
MEOW!

HUH! YOU MIGHT HAVE WAITED!

YOU AGAIN!

NEXT TIME I CATCH YOU CLIMBING A LAMP STANDARD, YOU'RE FOR IT!

TOWN COUNCIL OFFICE
I'LL TAKE A JOB TO KEEP ME OUT OF TROUBLE!
HELP WANTED

WN CIL CE
HUH! I DON'T KNOW IF IT WILL KEEP ME OUT OF TROUBLE!

SEE WHAT I MEAN? I'M A LAMP STANDARD CLEANER!
I WARNED YOU! NAME AND ADDRESS, PLEASE!

DAVID

THIS is the story of a shepherd lad who became one of the most famous kings in history. David, the youngest of the eight sons of Jesse, was tending his father's sheep in the hill country near Bethlehem when a lion attacked the flock.

The lion shall not have my father's lamb!

I must not be afraid. . .

Now is my chance to strike.

The lamb is not badly hurt. I will return it to its mother.

On another occasion, with no other weapon but his knife, David fought and killed a savage bear to save one of his father's sheep. The young boy's courage and fighting skill were to stand him in good stead in the years that lay ahead . . .

About this time, King Saul, the ruler of Israel, had led his army to a victory over the Amalekites and was returning home in triumph. Saul had made a prisoner of Agag, the King of the Amalekites, and also brought with him the pick of the enemy's cattle and sheep.

BENJAMIN

Samuel, the High Priest of Israel, halted the jubilant procession.

What is the meaning of this?

We have destroyed the Amalekites, sparing only Agag and the herds.

Nothing should have been spared! Agag is an evil man, for whom death is the only punishment. Bring him to me.

All your evil life you have shown no mercy. Now no mercy shall be shown unto you.

At his temple in Ramatha, Samuel meditated and prayed.

Finally—
God has shown me what I must do. I go to seek the man who will rule over Israel. The new king will unite the tribes of Israel. Our way lies south, in the hill country of Bethlehem.

When Samuel arrived at Bethlehem—
I wish to see the family of the chieftain named Jesse. God has chosen one of Jesse's sons to be your king.

I am Jesse. This is Eliab, my eldest son.
Eliab is indeed a big and handsome man, but he is not the one the Lord commands me to choose.

This son is not the chosen one either.

I have seen seven, and the chosen one is not among them. You have another son?
Only David, my youngest. He is herding the sheep.

At Samuel's command, David was sent for.
This youth is the one God called upon me to choose.

David, son of Jesse, you are now the Lord's anointed, to be King over Israel in days to come!

Samuel left, and David's way of life continued as if nothing had happened. Then, some months later, messengers arrived at Jesse's house.
We come hence from King Saul, and have journeyed far. The King demands that your son, David, be brought back by us to the Royal Court.
This is David, my youngest son. What does King Saul want of him?
The King is much troubled in spirit, and wants a musician to play to him. It is reported that your son, David, is much skilled in music.

You will take these customary gifts to the King, David—bread, and wine and a kid of the flock.

Later, at King Saul's palace—
The King is smiling. The music pleases him.

Saul honoured David by appointing him armour bearer—David carried his Royal master's spear and shield on ceremonial occasions.

When his brothers were called to the army to fight the Philistines, David had to return home to help on the farm.

Back home—
David, somebody is needed to take supplies to your brothers at the war. You will have to do the task.

When David reached the Israelite camp with his supplies, he was met by his brother Eliab.
Why did you come here? Was it so that you could see the battle?

"I will fight Goliath."

The giant Goliath attacked at once—
The Lord does not save with sword and spear. He will give you, Goliath, into our hands.
David loosed his sling—

My aim was true—the giant has fallen.
Die, Goliath!
Our champion is defeated. Flee!

Attack! Attack!
The youth who killed Goliath, the Philistine, has given us this great victory!

After the battle, King Saul summoned David.
Whose son are you, young man?
I am the son of Jesse of Bethlehem, as you know, sire.

Later—
David's fame and popularity worry me. For he is one of the people of Judah, who are against me.
David, I give you these as a token of friendship.
Jonathan, son of King Saul, I greet you.

When Saul's army returned from the war, there was great rejoicing.
Saul has slain his thousands and David his tens of thousands.
What more can this David have but my kingdom itself?

Later, as David played for the jealous king—
I shall slay this young upstart with my javelin!

But David spotted Saul's move and ducked.

The months went by and David was still kept under watch by the King. He made no further attempt on the youth's life, but when David was old enough to become an officer of the army—
Let him be sent out on a specially dangerous mission against the Philistines. Then perhaps he will be killed!

The King's scheme failed. David was successful in several different battles with the Philistines, and his reputation grew greater throughout Israel.

Father, why do you hate David so? He has done you no harm.
Let him return to court and I will be his friend.

When David returned to the palace, he was popular with everyone—except Saul.
We have heard great stories of your deeds of bravery, David.

And later the jealous King made another attempt on the youth's life—

This time, David had to get right out of Saul's power. He sought out Samuel, the High Priest of Israel.
It is David. As I expected, he has quarrelled with Saul. This is the beginning of the civil war which will eventually make David King of Israel.

THE ROAD TO CALVARY

LONG ago, in the land of Israel, a man came to be baptised in the River Jordan by the prophet, John the Baptist. The man's name was Jesus.

When He left the water after being baptised, the Heavens opened and a voice said, "Thou art my beloved Son, in whom I am well pleased."

The voice bade Jesus go into the wilderness for 40 days, where He prayed, endured hardships and gained strength for the ordeal which was to come.

Meanwhile John the Baptist's preaching had annoyed King Herod and the prophet was arrested and thrown into prison.

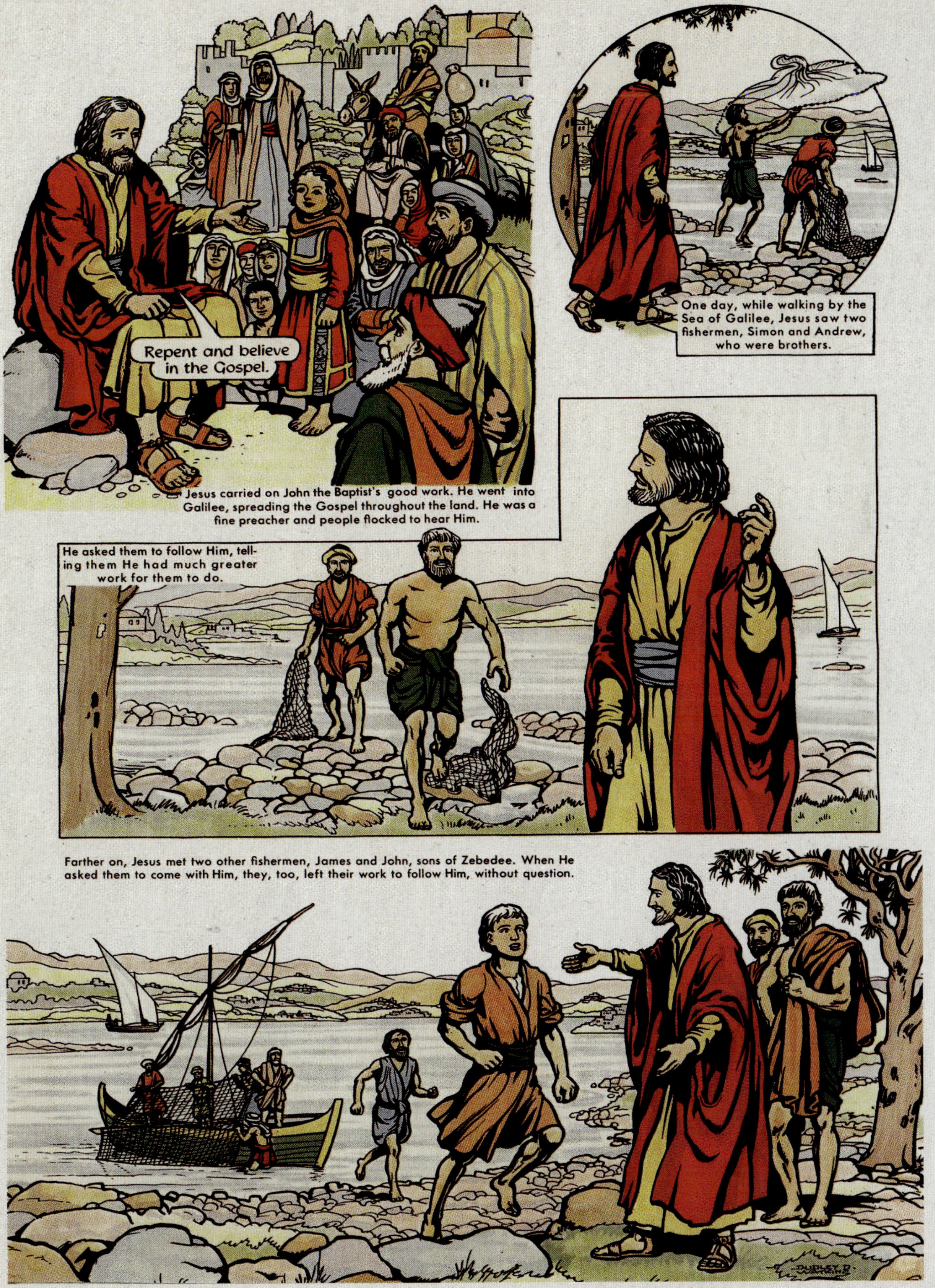

Jesus carried on John the Baptist's good work. He went into Galilee, spreading the Gospel throughout the land. He was a fine preacher and people flocked to hear Him.

One day, while walking by the Sea of Galilee, Jesus saw two fishermen, Simon and Andrew, who were brothers.

He asked them to follow Him, telling them He had much greater work for them to do.

Farther on, Jesus met two other fishermen, James and John, sons of Zebedee. When He asked them to come with Him, they, too, left their work to follow Him, without question.

Jesus took His new followers into Capernaum, where a great crowd gathered to hear Him preach. Four men brought a paralysed man to see Jesus, but could not get near Him.
Please let us through!
So they broke through the roof above Jesus and lowered the man in. Jesus forgave the man's sins and told him to stand up and walk.
I can walk!
Priests and lawyers who watched, said Jesus' words were blasphemy, as only God could forgive sins. But Jesus did give the man back the power to walk.

Some Pharisees rebuked Jesus one Sabbath for letting His men pluck corn, as it was against the Sabbath Law. But Jesus told them that the laws weren't made to penalise men. His men were hungry and had to eat.
On another Sabbath, Pharisees took Jesus to task for restoring a man's withered arm in a Synagogue. But Jesus asked them whether it was better to do good or evil on the Sabbath, to save life or kill. They had no answer to that question.
He usurps our authority!
We must get rid of Him!
It seemed to the Pharisees that Jesus was making a mockery of their strict laws.
But Jesus carried on with His work and soon He had gathered around Him twelve men, chosen to travel the land with Him, preaching the Gospel and serving God.

The Bullying Drummer

THE shrill cries of a dog in pain echoed through a little birch wood in the heart of the Scottish Highlands. Mingled with the howling of the dog came shouts of anger and the loud crack of a whip.

"Take that, you brute!" a breathless voice rang out. "And that—and that—and that!"

With each fiercely-uttered word came another crack of the whip.

At the edge of the wood Wild Young Dirky, the famous boy outlaw, came to a sudden halt and stood listening for a moment. Dirky's dark eyes flashed angrily as he realised what the sounds meant. Plunging into the wood, he raced through between tall tree-trunks and burst into a little clearing.

There, tied to a tree in the middle of the wood, was a gaunt black and white dog. Standing over it, with a heavy whip in his hand, stood a tall, sly-looking youth of about seventeen, wearing the uniform of a drummer in King George's Redcoat Army. There was a cruel look on his face as he swung the whip at the cringing dog.

"Take that!" he yelled again. "Take that, you brute!" And down came the whip across the dog's back.

Wild Young Dirky wasn't going to stand for that. In an instant he dropped the sack he was carrying. Next moment his hand streaked to one of the dirks which he carried in a bandolier slung across his chest. As the drummer raised his whip to hit the dog another blow, Dirky's wrist jerked, and the razor-edged weapon sped like an arrow through the air.

The blade of the dirk went clean through the lash of the whip and cut it in two. Then, flashing on, the dirk drove deep into the trunk of a birch tree beyond.

The drummer whirled round with fear in his eyes, and stared in amazement at the sturdy figure of the boy outlaw.

"Wild Young Dirky!" he breathed.

It was not surprising that the young Redcoat recognised the boy outlaw, for there was a price on Dirky's head. In those early months of 1746, the Redcoat armies were preparing for a final assault on the Highlanders who had risen in support of Bonnie Prince Charlie. Dirky was a thorn in the flesh of King George's men. Indeed, his description had been circulated to every troop of Redcoat soldiers in the north, and many a Redcoat eagerly sought the reward offered for the capture of the youngster, whose skill as a dirk-thrower had earned him his name of Wild Young Dirky.

Drummer Gurney was no fool. He knew all this, and now he saw a chance to earn himself the reward.

A sharp shock for Drummer Gurney!

"If only I can get close enough to hit him !" he thought craftily. But he gave no outward sign of what he was thinking. Whatever he did, he must not arouse Dirky's suspicion.

"I don't know who you are," he hissed scornfully, " but that dog is my dog, and I can do what I like with him. When he don't obey me, I thrash him !"

The tall drummer took a step closer to Dirky.

"My name's Ben Gurney," he went on, " and I say it's no business of you Highlanders what. . . ."

Suddenly, he broke off, raised his head, and stared as if in fright at something behind Dirky.

"Look out !" cried Ben Gurney.

Taken off guard, Dirky whirled round to see what had scared the drummer. For once, he had allowed himself to be tricked. Before he knew where he was, Gurney was on him, with lowered head and flailing fists. Punches rained on Dirky from all directions.

Thud !   Thud !   Through the tough cloth of Gurney's uniform the dirks sped, and drove deep into the trunk of the tree. In a moment the drummer was pinned there helplessly, and the panting Dirky stood in triumph before his enemy.

Using the severed whip lash, Dirky bound Gurney's hands and feet to the tree. Then he stuck his dirks back into their sheaths and set the dog free, patting it gently on the head.

"He can't get at you now," he said softly, as the dog cringed away.

Then, ignoring pleas by Gurney to be set free, Dirky picked up his sack. With swinging stride, he passed through the trees, and in a few moments was finally lost to sight. Ben Gurney was left alone.

But now a strange thing happened. Dirky was scarcely out of sight when the black and white dog slunk forward and crept to its master's feet.

Drummer Gurney seemed to have the advantage — but young Dirky wasn't beaten yet !

Toe-to-toe, the two lads stood and fought. In such a scrap, Dirky could normally give a good account of himself, even against opponents bigger and stronger than himself. But the early, unexpected hail of punches thrown by Gurney had dazed him, and he was knocked to the ground. Gurney dived on top of him, and the two lads rolled over and over before Dirky managed to break free. With a great effort he staggered to his feet.

As the drummer boy rushed at him again, Dirky's hand flew to his belt of dirks.

Swish ! Through the air flew one of his shining weapons. Gurney felt a sharp tug at his upraised right arm. He was whirled round off balance, as if caught by some invisible hand, and hurled against the trunk of one of the birch trees. His right sleeve was pinned to the tree by the dirk.

Before Gurney realised what was happening, Dirky's hands sped again to his belt. His dirks flew through the air like streaks of lightning.

Then, in spite of all the cruel treatment it had received from Gurney, the dog began to gnaw at the bonds round his ankles.

Soon it had chewed right through the tough leather, and Gurney's legs were freed. Then the clever dog reared up on its hindlegs and began to gnaw at the bonds holding Gurney's arms. It quickly bit through them, and Ben Gurney was free.

The young Redcoat showed little gratitude for his dog's loyalty.

" There's some use in you after all," he snarled, lashing out with his foot at the underfed animal. " And now to see if I can find the hiding place of that Highland brat !"

Breathing heavily, Gurney sneaked cautiously through the wood in the direction Dirky had taken. His dog kept its distance, wary of more harsh treatment from its cruel master.

The drummer had not gone far when a gleam of triumph came into his piggy little eyes.

In the cave of many weapons.

Dirky didn't know that his meal-sack was leaking —

"Here's a clue !" he muttered, with an evil grin.

There, on the ground before him, was a track that could not be mistaken—a track that would lead him to Young Dirky's hiding-place. It was a faint trail of oatmeal.

The Oatmeal Trail

UNKNOWN to Dirky, there was a tiny hole in the bottom of the sack he was carrying. As he moved through the wood, a thin trickle of oatmeal was falling from the hole and sprinkling the ground behind him. Along that trail, his heart beating with excitement, the drummer followed Dirky. Gurney's cunning brain was working fast as he followed the boy outlaw.

At any ordinary time Drummer Gurney would have been too scared to go far from the castle where his company was garrisoned. But the thought of finding Dirky's hiding-place spurred him on. If he could learn where it was, he would lead a Redcoat patrol to the spot and claim the reward offered for Dirky's capture.

Through woods and heather, over rocks and torrents, Gurney followed the trail. At last, panting triumphantly, he found himself at the cunningly-concealed entrance to a big cave—one of Dirky's many hiding-places as he moved across the country on secret missions for the Highland army.

Peering cautiously through the entrance to the cave, Gurney spied on the boy outlaw. Dirky had reached the cave several minutes before, and was now lighting a fire in the middle of the floor, ready to prepare a meal for himself.

It was not the sight of Dirky alone that caused Gurney's heart to leap with triumph. It was the glimpse he got of an amazing array of weapons contained in the cave. All round the walls hung swords and pikes and daggers, fire-arms and shields, and at the back of the cave there was even a little brass cannon. There, too,

were several barrels which looked as though they might be full of gunpowder.

What the drummer did not know about the weapons was that they were nearly a hundred years old, broken and rusty and useless. They had once been captured from Oliver Cromwell's men by a force of Highlanders, who had later abandoned them in the cave.

But Gurney thought he had made a discovery. "An arms store !" he muttered. "Arms for the men of the rebel army !   This will mean an even bigger reward for me, if I can get away without that young savage seeing me."

Step by step, Gurney retreated from the mouth of the cave.   Only when he was safely behind cover did he start to run, racing for the Redcoat-occupied castle as fast as his legs could carry him. By the time he reached the castle, he was breathless and trembling.

"I must see the colonel at once, sir," he gasped to the first officer he met.   "I've discovered a secret arms store in a cave—and Wild Young Dirky is there, too. If a patrol leaves here right away, we can capture him !"

The officer promptly whisked him off to the colonel's room, and there the excited drummer boy blurted out his story again.

The colonel made up his mind quickly.

"Is the young outlaw alone there meantime?" he demanded.

"Yes, sir—he's all alone," replied Drummer Gurney.

"Then we must move quickly," the colonel declared. "Rebel clansmen may already be on the way there to collect the weapons. Sergeant—you will take charge of a patrol !"

"Yes, sir," replied the sergeant.

"Take a score of men and a waggon," the colonel commanded.   "Drummer Gurney will lead you to the cave.   Capture Young Dirky, collect every weapon you find there, and return to the barracks. I want to question that boy. A

—but Drummer Gurney did, for he found the oatmeal trail.

good flogging may open the young savage's mouth. He knows every cave and track in the Highlands, and I'm certain he knows a great deal about the movements of the rebel army. We may get important news from him. Is that clear?"

" Yes, sir," said the sergeant.

" Then off with you," snapped the colonel. " The sooner the job is done the better. Take every precaution against ambush."

A Shoal of Redcoats!

THE Redcoat patrol, headed by Gurney and his dog, set off at a steady trot from the castle. But a mile away from the cave where Dirky had settled down for the night, the dog suddenly put its nose to the ground and sniffed eagerly. Then it darted away ahead.

" What's wrong with that brute?" cried the sergeant. " If it gives the alarm—— !"

" I think it's after a rabbit," broke in Gurney.

But Gurney was wrong. Patch, the dog, was not after a rabbit. It had come on Wild Young Dirky's scent, and it remembered the strange boy who had saved it from a whipping. Yelping joyously, it bounded ahead, following the scent and making straight for Dirky's cave.

The Redcoats moved on without the dog, and presently Gurney held up a hand.

" The cave is not far distant—yonder, up on the hillside," he said.

" We'll leave the waggon here," snapped the sergeant. " We must go forward carefully in case any Highlanders are lying in wait for us !"

Up in the cave, Dirky started up from his bed of bracken with a cry of alarm. A warm, wet tongue was slobbering over his face. Snuffling and whining, Patch had roused the boy from his sleep.

The skinny animal leaped up on him, barking joyously, showing every sign of delight. Then suddenly it bounded away from the cave and disappeared down the hillside.

The dog's last action warned Dirky. In a moment he was wide-awake. Dirky guessed— rightly—that the dog's presence could mean only one thing. Drummer Gurney was not far away !

Dirky ran to the entrance of the cave, and peered out into the night. He could see nothing, but down the hillside he heard the barking of a dog. Suddenly its barking changed to a yelp of pain, and Dirky understood. He knew that someone had struck the dog.

That person had been the sergeant.

" Shut up, you yelping brute !" he snarled at Patch, kicking the animal cruelly. Then on he crept, following young Gurney, the rest of the Redcoats crawling after them.

Like a shadow, Dirky stole away from the cave. Not far from the entrance was a thick clump of heather, and Dirky made straight for it. He grasped a heather bush with his hand, and pulled. The heather lifted clear of the ground, in spite of the fact that he used little effort to pull it up. That heather had no roots. It was fixed to the lid of a barrel that was sunk into the peaty turf.

The boy dropped down into the barrel, and let the heather-covered lid fall on top of him just as Gurney, leading the soldiers, came into sight.

" There's the cave," whispered the drummer to the sergeant.

For a few moments the soldiers stood stock-still, listening intently. Then the sergeant bellowed the order—" *Charge !*"

With a wild howl, the Redcoats raced for the entrance to the cave. Gurney's feet thudded on top of Dirky's barrel-lid as he passed, but the drummer noticed nothing unusual.

" Surrender !" yelled Gurney, bursting into the cave. " Surrender or——"

But his voice died away.

" There's no one here," he ended lamely. " He's gone !"

Into the cave crowded the soldiers, peering all round the place, which was dimly lit up by

To outwit the advancing Redcoats, the boy outlaw was going underground !

It was the best catch Dirky had ever made—a whole shoal of Redcoats!

Dirky's fire. They eyed the weapons on the wall, and suddenly the sergeant turned to Gurney with an angry cry. He grabbed the drummer by the scruff of the neck and shook him as a terrier shakes a rat.

"So this is what you brought us all the way from the castle for !" he roared. "Strike me blue ! Half the weapons here are as old as the hills. Most of these guns wouldn't fire ! And where's the young cur that's supposed to be here? Where is he, I ask you?"

Pushing up the lid of his barrel, Dirky listened, chuckling to himself. The Redcoats were moving about inside the cave, looking around the place curiously. Cat-like, Dirky scrambled out of the barrel and stole to the side of the cave-mouth. There, hung out to dry on a rock face, was a fishing net that he had been using only the previous day to catch fish in the big mountain loch at the foot of the glen. Working quickly and silently, Dirky removed it from the rock, and strung it up between two tall birch trees growing right in front of the cave entrance. One part hung down between the two trees like a curtain— the net itself was supported by a thin cord stretched from trunk to trunk. Now, with drawn

dirk, Dirky moved out of sight behind one of the trees, ready to cut the cord bearing the weight of the net.

The boy outlaw cupped his hands round his mouth, and yelled a battle cry often used by Prince Charlie's men.

"The White Cockade for ever !" he roared at the pitch of his voice. "They're trapped. Death to the Redcoats. Hooray for the White Cockade !"

"An ambush !" choked the Redcoat sergeant. "Out, lads—out, or we'll be trapped like rats. Out ! Down with the rebels !"

Bayonet thrust out in front of him, expecting at any moment a bullet in the chest from Highland marksmen, he charged for the entrance and the darkness beyond. Headlong he rushed into the unseen barrier before him. As the net halted his progress, his men, stumbling behind, came crashing into him in a solid body. In that second, Dirky slashed through the cord supporting the bulging net. Down it fell, the top part dropping behind the pack of trapped Redcoats, completely enveloping them. They were caught like a shoal of fish, and the more they struggled, the more entangled they became in the great folds of the net.

Wild Young Dirky's gunpowder plot!

Wild Young Dirky gave a great shout of laughter. Leaping past the yelling bundle of men, he hurried into the cave. Then he rolled one of the gunpowder kegs to the entrance of the cave, staved in the top of it, and snatched a blazing brand from the fire.

"Surrender!" he yelled. "Surrender or I'll blow you all to pieces."

The threat was enough. Although the barrel was empty, the Redcoats did not know that. Their struggles ceased, and all eyes watched Dirky's movements.

But meanwhile one of the soldiers had managed to escape from the net. A cry of terror broke from his lips, and he turned to flee. Before he could get more than three paces away Dirky sprang into action. Snatching up a stout cudgel, with one quick movement he threw it as he would throw a dirk, sending it thudding against the Redcoat's head. With a grunt the soldier collapsed in a limp heap on the ground.

Then Dirky waded into his closely-packed group of prisoners. Man after man he knocked on the head, as each Redcoat struggled to escape from the net through the opening that the first soldier had made with his knife. In a very short time every one of the soldiers was stretched out unconscious, including Drummer Gurney himself.

When the Redcoats came to their senses, it was to find their hands tightly bound behind them. As they staggered to their feet, Dirky blindfolded them with strips of their own shirts, so that they could see nothing. Then, forming them into file at the point of a dirk, he gave the order to march, guiding the leading men with a strip of rawhide.

Dirky had decided against attempting to take his prisoners to the nearest Highland camp, many miles distant. But he kept the breathless Redcoats on the move for hours, forcing them up rocky slopes, and through great stretches of bog. Finally, in the heart of the hills, he halted them.

"You will give me five minutes to get clear," he ordered. "Then you are free to return to your headquarters. Your night's exercise will do you good!"

And with that, the boy outlaw slipped off like a shadow. But he did not go far. Dodging into hiding behind a big boulder nearby, he crouched there, waiting and listening.

When at last the Redcoats felt certain they were alone, and struggled to drag the bandages from each other's eyes, they found they had an all-night walk in front of them to reach their headquarters.

The Redcoats were furious—and none more so than their sergeant.

Now he grabbed Drummer Gurney by the shoulder and glared at the trembling youth.

"You will be held responsible for leading us into the trap!" he grated. "I promise you a flogging you will not forget for a lifetime, my lad!"

Crouching unseen behind the boulder, Wild Young Dirky chuckled softly in approval.

"Well he deserves it," he muttered. "It is a just punishment for anyone who would treat a poor dog as he did."

As he spoke, he became aware of something soft and warm licking the back of his hand. With a sudden start, he looked round, and there was Patch, the dog he had saved from a thrashing, crouching beside him.

Young Dirky's eyes flashed with delight.

"Good boy—good boy," he whispered, patting the hound's head. "Stay with me, and I will look after you. You and I together will lead the Redcoats many a fine dance!"

The dog growled deep in its throat in a contented way and snuggled closer to its new master. Wild Young Dirky had found a true friend to share his wanderings and adventures.

Watkins' final Biffo the Bear would be published on the 25th of October, 1969. Only half finished, it was completed by Watkins' friend and fellow legendary DC Thomson artist, David Sutherland.

"When I was aware of Dudley D Watkins' talent I was in transition from advertising to hopefully becoming a comic illustrator. It became apparent that Dudley was not only a fantastic picture artist, but a superb and prolific cartoonist with well-known titles to his credit! After many years of studying Dudley's artwork I am still in awe and jealous of his ability to encompass such a diversity of subjects with such apparent ease!

I am one of many artists in this "field" to tip their berets to the talents and mastery of Dudley D Watkins."

With sincerity, David Sutherland

The Beano
4D
EVERY THURSDAY
No. 1423—October 25th, 1969.

BIFFO THE BEAR
HELLO, BUSTER! HA-HA! IT'S AN AWFUL DAY! TEE-HEE!
WHAT'S HE SO HAPPY ABOUT?

HERE'S MY BUTCHER'S BILL — HO-HO! — MY MILKMAN'S BILL — HAW-HAW!

TEE-HEE! THE LIGHT'S FUSED! HO-HO!
CLICK!

HA-HA-HA!

CACKLE!

SNIGGER!

CHUCKLE!
GUFFAW!
CHORTLE!
HE'S POTTY!

I'D BETTER FIND OUT WHAT'S GOING ON!
BIFFO

THIS — HA-HA! — NEW HAIRY CARPET OF MINE — TEE-HEE! — ISN'T HALF TICKLY! HAW-HAW!
TICKLE
TICKLE

DUDLEY D WATKINS

Dudley D Watkins worked at DC Thomson 1925–1969.

We hope we have shed some light on the career of the genius behind some of the most beloved characters in British comics history. Dudley D Watkins created some of the loudest belly-laughs and guffaws generation after generation, laying the foundations for what Beano, The Dandy and The Sunday Post are to this day.

COW PIE
(TINY)

HERE WE ARE, GANG!
NOT A BAD LITTLE PLACE, EH?
OOH — LET'S SEE THE MACHINES.
HELP — YOU'RE SHOVING US OVER!
GEE! SORRY, SNATCH!
PRINTING INK
THAT AS
AS FOR YOU, SNOOTY — YOU CAN WORK OUT "THE BEANO" ACCOUNTS. 5,000,000 BEANOS AT 2d EACH, 19560 TONS OF PAPER AT 5¾d A POUND!
— AND YOU, SCRAPPER — CAN BE THE DOORMAN — SKINNY LIZZIE AND ROSIE, YOU ARE TO WORK THE LIFTS — HAPPY HUTTON, YOU ARE OFFICE BOY AND YOU, HAIRPIN, SWEEP THE FLOOR!